Bryan Foster

Love is the Meaning of Life: GOD'S Love

(1st ed.)

Bryan Foster

Love is the Meaning of Life: GOD'S Love

(Author Articles)

(1st ed.)

Book 6 of the 'GOD Today' Series

Bryan Foster

GREAT DEVELOPMENTS Publishers

Bryan Foster

Published in 2021
Great Developments Publishers
Gold Coast, Queensland, Australia 4217
ABN: 13133435168 USA-EIN: 98-0689457

Creator: Foster, Bryan, 1957- author, publisher, director

 A catalogue record for this book is available from the National Library of Australia

Title: Love is the Meaning of Life: GOD's Love

ISBN: (hardback)   978-0-6489520-0-8
ISBN: (paperback)   978-0-6489520-1-5
ISBN: (large print paperback) 978-0-6489520-2-2
ISBN: (ebook)   978-0-6489520-3-9

Notes: Includes bibliographical references and index.

'GOD Today' Series:

1GOD.world: One GOD for All, (Author Articles) (2016)

Mt Warning GOD's Revelation: Photobook Companion to '1GOD.world', (2017)

Where's GOD? Revelations Today, (Author Articles) (2018)

Where's GOD? Revelations Today Photobook Companion: GOD Signs (2ⁿᵈed) (2018) **Author's favourite**.

Jesus and Mahomad are GOD (Author Articles) (2020)

Love is the Meaning of Life: GOD'S Love (1ˢᵗ ed) (Author Articles) (2021)

Author's Websites:

https://www.GodTodaySeries.com/
https://www.BryanFosterAuthor.com/
https://www.JesusAndMahomadAreGod.com/ (Developing)
https://www.LoveIsTheMeaningOfLife.com/ (Developing)

+ various social media webpages

Images in the 'GOD Today' Series:

Bryan and Karen Foster (GDP) and Andrew Foster (Austographer.com)
Copyright © 2020 Cover photo by Bryan Foster:
Moonrise at Palm Beach, Gold Coast, Australia
Graphics: Bryan Foster and Bookpod

Bryan Foster

DEDICATION

Dedicated to Karen, the Love of my life, my wife of 42 years.
My rock, my Uluru, my heart of Australia.
And to my children Leigh-Maree, Andrew and Jacqui, daughter-in-law Shannon and grandchildren Kyan, Cruze, Felicity and Isabella.
To my parents, Frank (deceased 2018) and Mary.
And to my siblings John, Susy and Clare and all my extended family.
Thank you for all your Love, support and encouragement.
To my dear friends and education colleagues, thank you.

CONTENTS

WHAT is LOVE? Some everyday answers

LOVE IS THE MEANING OF LIFE:

GOD'S LOVE

ABSOLUTE LOVE of GOD

GOD and PRAYER

GOD, Us and LOVE

GOD's LOVE

Where is GOD's LOVE?

RELIGIOUS - LOVE CHALLENGES TODAY

LOVE'S CHALLENGES for GOD's PEOPLE

RELIGIOUS – LOVE CHALLENGES TODAY

RELIGIOUS - LOVE SOLUTIONS TODAY

GOD's SPECIAL LOVING GIFTS for US

Bryan Foster

AUTHOR'S 42 YEARS TEACHING

CONCLUSION   303

APPENDICES

(*Mahomad was spelt this way by GOD during the
revealing of the Revelations in May 2016.)

Each book in this *'GOD Today' Series* invites us in various ways to join in the discovery of GOD, GOD's Revelations, Inspired Messages and Love, as we journey towards our own personal and communal salvation with GOD on Earth and later in Heaven.

We can accept that this relationship with GOD is the most positive, enhancing, honest, forgiving, and absolutely loving one we could ever imagine.

The closer we get to the Absolutely Loving GOD, the closer we can find out about our true soulful selves.

We find out that GOD's divine relationship with us all is so much more significant and impressive than for one we could forever imagine.

Each quote in these grey boxes is from this book by author, Bryan Foster.

Each quote is Copyright © 2021 by

Bryan W Foster.

Foreword by Karen Foster

I have been blessed to have witnessed Bryan's close contact with GOD for many years. His primary purpose is to help as many people as possible find GOD in their lives as he has been fortunately able to do himself. This latest book in the *'GOD Today'* *Series*, Book 6, titled, *Love, is the Meaning of Life: GOD's Love*, 2021, shares the absolute necessity for real Love in today's world. It details the world's connection to the Absolutely Loving, One and Only GOD forever.

Bryan invites you to explore fascinating and affirming messages from GOD and about GOD for today's world for each of us in our own particular and necessary way. We all need GOD's Love and guidance to help our earthly lives prepare for meeting GOD in Heaven, after our time on Earth comes to an end.

This sixth book in Bryan's *'GOD Today'* *Series* continues the journey of discovering GOD's Love that began with *1GOD.world: One GOD for All* in 2016.

Each book in this *'GOD Today'* *Series* invites us to join in the discovery of GOD; GOD's Revelations, GOD's inspired messages and GOD's Love, as we journey towards our own personal and communal salvation with GOD in Heaven.

This relationship with GOD is the most positive, enhancing, honest, forgiving, and absolutely loving one we could ever imagine. The closer we get to the Absolutely Loving GOD, the more we find out about our true soulful selves and GOD.

GOD truly is the trendsetter on Love, REAL Love. Nothing comes close to GOD's Absolute Love. We need to treat ourselves and others – lovingly. This then draws us more to - GOD.

It is highly recommended that readers view the previous photobook before this next book. It contains the surprising and unique sun, cloud and moon images taken by Bryan. These help the reader be inspired to search for GOD and GOD's messages for each of us. In photobook, Book 4, *Where's GOD? Revelations Today Photobook Companion: GOD Signs* there challenging photographic images taken by the author and gifted by GOD. These help to bring us to a much closer place with GOD. *Each is genuine, real, unique, exciting and also possibly quite challenging for the reader.* Many of these images certainly surprised us when seeing each for the first time. GOD jumps to the forefront of our lives. The associated text in the photobook, explain as best we can, God's images gifted to us and the world today. Book 4, is Bryan's favourite book in the *Series* as the photos are breathtaking and can't help but lead us towards GOD. *Enjoy the photos and be challenged with accepting GOD's Messages for us today!*

In this next book, *Love is the Meaning of Life: GOD'S Love,* Bryan renews and continues exploring who GOD is, but now *emphasises the Love Story of, and for, GOD, and us together as One.* What is GOD's Love? What is our Love? And how to be dependent and needing of GOD and each other, especially those close to us. We can then be open to how GOD is discovered and followed in our lives and through our loving experiences.

(Karen and Bryan – have been married for 42 years. Religious Education teachers - Bryan for 42 years, Karen for 38 years.)

Preface

Love is the Meaning of Life: GOD's Love

We crave and aspire for the deepest kind of Love. This is God's, Absolute Love! The more we know God and God's creations and God's Absolute Love for each one of us, the closer we grow to God and others, which will eventually be what we are offered on death's doorstep. It will be our one last choice - GOD or Evil (No God).

Why is it so crucial that humanity has a lifelong search for Love? Do we properly understand Love? Why does Love mean so much that most people work extremely hard on our loving relationships, gain, then keep and develop these, if we want to be in Love? There are a variety of love types. Many will be explored in this book.

Why does Love so agree with us that most of us continue to improve our relationships so as to meet true Love daily, hourly, by the minute, or even by the second when it counts as a necessity?

Why do we 'fear' not having Love and work intensely for this not to happen? What is missing when Love goes? Is it God whom we forced away? How does it go? Does God take it away, or do we move it away from us through our beliefs and actions being non-loving?

WE do the moving away! God is permanently there for us. It is our behaviour and beliefs we live by, which keeps us close to God or pushes us away. We control our destiny with GOD's help. It is our personal choice at our death.

Why are we here on Earth? Why did God create us all to exist here? Not just those alive now but the billions before us and the billions to follow us? Is this God's Will/plan?

Our intention is eventuating from how we live on this most majestic creation, Earth, along with our relationships with people, but most importantly – with GOD! We must Love God ahead of anything else. God first – people second! Not forgetting that the way we love our humanity and those close to God is essential for all humanity to move towards God at our death moment and then choose God not evil to exist forever.

We might not be aware that the Love we search for is always there waiting for us, but just needing our acknowledgement and request to become one with us. That most incredible Loving feeling and response to everything is GOD! The Love we search for -

IS GOD! GOD IS LOVE!

That is, God's perfect Love! It is not of our world but can be attained to a degree in this world. It is from God to us on Earth. We live for GOD now, and GOD then brings us close with 'Him', while on Earth. Directly from God's world to us in this world. And then to be progressed to experiencing the Absolute of God's Love in Heaven after our deaths!

God's Love is what LOVE is all about! We come to Love in our relationships with God and other humans through our Godly Loving experiences and relationships.

God shares with us 'His' genuine and authentic LOVE. This includes our forgiveness sort from God and others. We can become ONE with GOD at our death if we choose this to be our way as we die! God's Love meets Our Love. If genuine, we live forever with GOD! Our final beliefs are critical for eternity!!!

'GOD Today' Series - Overviews

A series of nine books, i.e. six texts and three photobooks, along with a video series by Bryan Foster, released between 2016 and 2021/2.

Book 1. 1GOD.world: One GOD for All (Author Articles) (2016)

Book 2. Mt Warning GOD's Revelation: Photobook Companion to '1GOD.world' (2017)

Book 3. Where's GOD? Revelations Today (Author Articles) (2018)

Book 4. Where's GOD? Revelations Today Photobook Companion: GOD Signs (1ˢᵗ & 2ⁿᵈ ed.'s) (2018)

'GOD Today' Video Series (2018)

Book 5. Jesus and *Mahomad are GOD (Author Articles) (2020)

Book 6. Love is The Meaning of Life: GOD'S Love (Author Articles) (1ˢᵗ ed.) (2021)

Book 7. Love is The Meaning of Life (Author Articles) (2ⁿᵈ ed.) (2021) OUT 2021

Book 8. Wisdom of Love: Wisdom of GOD's Love (Author Articles) (Working Copy & Title) (2021/2) OUT 2021

Book 9. Love is The Meaning of Life GOD's Love: Photobook Companion (2021/2) OUT 2021/2

(*Mahomad spelt this way by GOD in the 2016 Revelations.)

1GOD.world: One GOD for All introduced in detail the first major Revelation from GOD for today and challenged the reader to search and find GOD through other people, nature and GOD's Revelations and inspired messages. It introduced the author to the reader and shared twenty-six of his personal, spiritual, finding-GOD stories, which will hopefully encourage and assist others in seeking and finding GOD. A series of inspired messages discerned by the author over his lifetime was shared. (See Appendix 1 for Contents.) **OUT NOW**

Mt Warning GOD's Revelation: Photobook Companion to '1GOD.world' is a 72-kilometre photographic exploration around Mt Warning and up to the walking track's starting point. These were taken over three years, culminating with the Revelations from GOD on the plains at the foot of the mountain one cold winter's night. It is a photographic and written story of the spectacular and spiritually inspiring Mt Warning and its surrounding towns, landscapes and fauna. Images are taken from most angles around its 72km base plus the road up to the walking track. – **OUT NOW**

Where's GOD? Revelations Today invites the reader to continue the journey of exploring who and where GOD is for them and what are GOD's messages for today's world. It details the twelve Revelations from GOD for today introduced in the previous two books. A collection of another six inspired messages received within that same 24-hour revelation period is shared. A key focus is on assisting the reader in their appreciation, understanding and searches for GOD in today's world. – **OUT NOW**

Where's GOD? Revelations Today Photobook Companion: GOD Signs surprises the reader with some exceptional, different and unique photographic images, possibly formed from various reflections and refractions of the sun or perhaps given directly from GOD. Some formed across the author, along with spectacular sunshine shapes formed in the sky. Especially look in the images presented for sun-formed arrows, flares, huge Easter sun cross, rainbows and cloud formations. These occurred at venues on the plains of, and at the foot of, Mt Warning, Cabarita and Kingscliff beaches, and Straddie, at Cylinder Beach, North Stradbroke Island and inland at Texas on the Queensland/New South Wales border. The sun is seen as central for many people to imagine and discerning GOD and GOD's beyond-our-reality's extraordinary powers. Other spectacular sunrise and sunset images are shared. Our sun is the centre of our world – no sun, no lives. ** The photos are so genuinely striking and unique that this Book 4 is the author's favourite book.** These pictures tell thousands of words combined. - **OUT NOW**

Jesus and Mahomad are GOD was released in July 2020. A massive challenge for around fifty per cent of the world's population is issued. Both Jesus and Mahomad are the incarnate one and only GOD. Revelation #15 is this book's title. Prayer and relationships with GOD and the incarnate GOD hold critical possibilities for our future world. The first and possibly overawing Revelation that is the basis for this book came during the Revelations from GOD to the author in May 2016. The world will be religiously challenged like possibly no other time in history. The extremists and the violent must remain faithful and peaceful, no matter their likely strong desire to do otherwise. No excuse! Our loving, most peaceful GOD allows for nothing else. GOD won't accept any violence, especially in 'His' name! One essential outcome becomes the divine example of GOD's Love – we are all equal and holy before GOD until we sin. Forgiveness from us is then required. A most profound and exemplary reality of GOD is the Incarnations of Jesus and Mahomad at different times in history. - **OUT NOW**

Love is The Meaning of Life: GOD'S Love (Author Articles) (*1ˢᵗ edition.*) is planned for release in early 2021. A significant exploration of what Love is and how it affects us all introduces this book and is the theme followed throughout. There is a major discussion on the types of Love, its positive and sometimes negative impacts, and how we can grow in true Love throughout our lifetimes with our special lovers, family, friends, colleagues and communities. GOD is seen as the Absolute Lover in its perfect sense, who loves us all equally and desires our perfect union on this Earth and ultimately with GOD in Heaven. GOD's Love and people's Love is explored in detail. (The 2ⁿᵈ edition precedes the 1ˢᵗ – an edited version of the 2ⁿᵈ ed.) - **OUT NOW**

Love is The Meaning of Life (Author Articles) (2ⁿᵈ edition) (2021). This second edition of the *Love is The Meaning of Life: God's Love (1st edition)* book, is without the considerable emphasis on GOD in this book just given. The language and discussions will be clear and non-complex, without the often found necessity by various writers to make the Author Articles convoluted, which leads to losing the level of appreciation of the topic on Love. Yet, because GOD is the perfect Love and needed for any loving relationship, there is a limited but necessary amount of discussion on this point. The author can never minimise GOD's Truth in any edition of these books. An accurate story/explanation of what Love is and its impact on our lives is explored. People often get confused when speaking of Love, as there are several types and levels of Love. GOD is Absolute Love and Love is what we are trying to gain continually throughout our lives! Circumstances change, and so do relationships. When we achieve this Love, we also gain God! It will be a book on Love for all people. - **OUT 2021**

Wisdom of Love: Wisdom of GOD's Love (Author Articles) (Working Title) is planned to be released in 2021. It is a unique encounter with some refreshingly insightful quotes and including some challenging ones, as well. These range across each person's lifetime and are linked as examples to that stage of the author's life. The bulk comes from the first 60 years of life. How these can help each of us will be the reader's challenge as we all progress through life. People who especially enjoy spiritual and human reflections will be drawn to many of the quotes. Each one encourages serious reflection and addition to our lexicon. These have been developed by the author and formed over these past 40 years. These should add or support each reader's quotes from God. Then shared with others as felt appropriate - **OUT 2021**

Love is The Meaning of Life GOD's Love: Photobook Companion (2021/2) will actively support the previous textbook through significant photographic images. Some beautiful and authentic reflections of our Love and our lives are the basis of this photobook. The images will sometimes be quite challenging. These will support each reader, as they discover various divine and life messages and support from GOD. Combined with multiple literary genres used to enhance or support the photos, this book will be strong encouragement for those wishing for more Love in their lives and the world. Its emphasis is on how GOD, being Absolute Love, can help the reader develop our GOD relationships. - **OUT 2021/2**

'GOD Today' Series (2016-2021/2)

by Bryan Foster

Published by Great Developments Publishers (Australia)

available from all good internet bookstores.

GOD is just waiting for us to say,

'YES!'

'YES, I can!'

'Yes, I want You GOD to be a major and substantial part of my life.'

'Yes, I want to be a significant part of you, GOD's existence, too!'

'I love GOD, and GOD loves me beyond anything I could imagine.'

The 'best kept secret' is to LOVE GOD above everything else!!!

GOD is seriously waiting for us to NEED GOD and to work so as to be as close as we possibly can to GOD!

Author

There is a significant need to bring GOD back to the front and centre of societal leadership decisions and growth. The secular society is often making uninformed, and non-divinely influenced decisions, which have unnecessary major impacts on the various world populations. What do we need from GOD? How can we gain this? What does each person need to do – for GOD's Love!

Bryan Foster, the author, has been married to Karen Foster for forty-two years. He taught for 42 years and held senior leadership positions in religious schools and his Church deanery and parishes. They have three adult children and four grandchildren. Their two eldest children are teachers in Catholic schools, as is Karen, while their third daughter has just graduated with a Science degree. Bryan and Karen are very much still very much in Love after forty-two years. So much genuine, authentic Love, that it seems so strange writing it.

The author now concentrates on his publications through his and Karen's *Great Developments Publications*. His many books, articles and other writings, videos and photography, are his mainstay now having retired from the teaching of classes from year 1 to 12 over his career. As a religion teacher in secondary/high school, he specifically taught Study of Religion to senior students in years 11 and 12 for 30 years.

His latest *Series* being written presently is the *'GOD Today' Series,* which began in 2016 after Bryan received 15 Revelations from GOD, one cool winter's night in May, 2016 while caravanning on Mt Warning's plains near Murwillumbah, NSW, Australia. During these Revelations, GOD requested Bryan to write the first book while caravanning around Mt Warning in NSW near the Queensland border. Mt Warning has taken on an extraordinary significance in this *Series*. It has been in view or close-by when God gives Bryan Revelations or Loving support for something essential or divine. The *Series* will conclude about 2021/2, following the timeline given to the author by GOD. This latest book is the sixth book that has so far been published in this *Series*. The writings include non-fiction books, photobooks, videos, websites, images and social networking sites.

The author has published twenty-three books since 2008 across three themes. The themes being: GOD Today; Marketing religious schools and churches; and photobooks with hints and tips videos for caravan/trailer beginners, along with suggestions in photobooks and videos for caravan and camping travellers throughout Australia - sharing the highlights of places to stay and things to see and do on the roads throughout Australia. There are 780+ videos on YouTube to view across the themes. These are free to watch videos at this stage (channel 'efozz1' on YouTube) cover the above areas through video vision.

Bryan has played a significant role in religious schools, parishes and deanery. He has been a primary/elementary schools' principal, twice, and an assistant principal for religious education in secondary/high school for ten years. He has been a president/secretary of Catholic parishes and deanery pastoral councils on the Gold Coast and Brisbane, Australia.

The decision to feature GOD in this Book 6 is crucial to any discussion on Love. In the first four books in this *Series,* the fifteen initial Revelations received from GOD by the author in 2016 have been emphasised. *This next book goes to the core of Love, and GOD's loving place in our world* – a more in-depth exploration of two essential May 2016 Revelations. This is along with Bryan's six Revelations from GOD in November 2018; once again, while camping near Mt Warning. These latest Revelations highlight what Love is and how Love has an impact on every individual and community. *There is also a challenge for the reader to consider the place of GOD, seriously, in all Loving relationships. After all, we were born out of GOD's Love for us.*

LOVE is from GOD. GOD is Absolute LOVE! Everything we know about Love and its impact on us comes from GOD. Every experience we have of Love is from GOD – is of GOD with us. It is GOD's Absolute Love encouraging us to grow together as one people, one world - together with the One and Only, GOD. Love is the Meaning of Life: GOD'S Love.

Uppermost is Bryan's desire to grow as close as humanly possible to GOD and to genuinely assist as many people as he can in their quest to GOD on Earth, in the first instance. Then to complete the story, it will be each of our final decisions on what we genuinely Love fully at the time of our death – i.e. GOD or Evil. Heaven awaits those who choose the Absolute Love with GOD. After death, how we present to GOD has already been formed through our chosen lifestyles and beliefs while living our earthly lives.

Bryan taught religion for 42 years before retiring from being a senior teacher of Religious Education, and other Religious Educational subjects, including Religion and Ethics. This teaching time was spent in religious schools in the city and country, Queensland, Australia. These past twelve years, Bryan and his wife Karen, also produced and published their books and videos while still teaching full-time, through their own publishing company, *Great Developments Publishers*. See in this Book 6 the titles written and published from the *'GOD Today' Series*, plus other works soon to come.

Bryan Foster

Academic Qualifications:

Master of Education (Religious Education) (ACU)
Bachelor of Education (ACU)
Graduate Diploma of Religious Education (ACU)
Diploma of Religious Education (IFE)
Diploma of Teaching (McAuley College)

ACU = Australian Catholic University – Brisbane and Sydney

IFE = Institute of Faith - Brisbane

LOVE is from GOD.

GOD IS ABSOLUTE LOVE!

Everything we know about LOVE and its impact on us, comes from GOD.

Every experience we have of LOVE is from GOD – and is of GOD with us.

It is GOD's ABSOLUTE LOVE encouraging us to grow together as One People, One World –

together with the One and Only, ONE – GOD for all religions!

Love is the Meaning of Life – GOD'S LOVE.

LOVE GOD! LOVE EACH OTHER!

BRING EVERYTHING TOGETHER –

as

ONE.

Author's Websites

For further information and reader response:

https://www.GODtodayseries.com/
- Main website for this Series, includes the regularly updated blog commenced in 2016

https://www.jesusandmahomadareGOD.com/
- Book 5 (Coming Soon)

https://www.bryanfosterauthor.com/
- Author's website

https://loveisthemeaningoflifegodslove.com (Coming Soon)

https://loveisthemeaningoflife.com (Coming Soon)

http://www.greatdevelopmentspublishers.com/
- Publisher's new webpage. (Original website started in 2007, closed 12/2018. New webpage now.)

https://www.facebook.com/groups/389602698051426/
- 1GOD.world Facebook

https://au.linkedin.com/in/bryanfoster
- LinkedIn

https://www.youtube.com/user/efozz1
- 780+ YouTube videos commenced in 2009. Themes - 'GOD Today' Series. Caravan/trailer hints and tips for beginners. Places to see and things to do, mainly in Australia.

https://twitter.com/1GODworld1
- Twitter

https://www.instagram.com/
- Instagram (1GODworld) (Development stage)

Introduction

What is Love?

Love is the Meaning of Life: GOD'S Love!

This next book, Book 6 of the *'GOD Today' Series*, is written with a whole new emphasis on GOD and GOD's LOVE for all of us – equally and forever, while on Earth, and in Heaven after our death.

This new book takes a considerably different approach to explain LOVE compared to most recent book publications by others on the same topic. Most publications these days emphasise that humanity and love are a crucial part of our daily lives, which, of course, it is. However, the new tact of this Book 6 is to bring in the creator of the universe, to the table of true Love. GOD is needed to be included in all loving relationships. Without the presence of the Absolute Loving GOD in any loving relationship, the shallower it could become. Love requires an essential place for GOD's presence.

Book 6 is primarily an 'Author's Articles' publication emphasising authentic, worldly, divinely and GODLY/GOOD articles by this book's author. These articles have now been collated into similarly themed chapters and have developed over many years. You are lovingly invited to become one with the articles as they invite and encourage us to become one with God and each other, in and with Love - God's and our's.

This Book 6 in the *'GOD Today' Series*, is a Book concentrating on the legitimate and essentials of Love, i.e. initially and ideally, it is essential to be truly in Love with GOD. GOD gives us the options with whom 'He' needs to be followed and agreed. Without our love for GOD and each other, Love cannot develop to the level required of God for us. If we decide to concentrate on a Love without GOD, we sell ourselves and others very short.

Where does this incredible attraction to love come from? The secular authors mostly leave GOD out of, or minimally in the mix. Possibly because they legitimately don't understand, don't appreciate or don't believe in GOD's place in Love or in fact believe in GOD. This is so unfortunate, especially given GOD's supreme position in creation and today's world - having a more profound and divine approach to Love, should be how we experience it.

Love is so attractive to every person who has ever existed, is living now, or is yet to come. Just as GOD is forever, so is Love! But what it means and how it affects each person can be different depending on their circumstances and lifestyle. Love is what every normal person is after! Sometimes they don't even know this is the case or even what it is, yet it is still their main priority in life. So much is there for us all. Love is the meaning of life for everyone who can understand and appreciate life, love and GOD. Love=GOD.

People are so attracted to Love that it can, and should, impact very considerably on their lives. People often don't even realise that Love isn't just Love. But Love is GOD. GOD gives each of us this Love to use positively and helps all humanity be the best they can and enjoy life and one another. We need to Love GOD beyond everything else and aim to be one with GOD forever while on this Earth and after we die in Heaven.

No GOD = No True, Deep, Absolute, Awesome Love!!!

If people can't or won't accept GOD's role in living and being the Love that GOD gave us to share with humanity, they are 'selling' each other short! People are not Love! People's relationships with each other are not entirely - Love! Only when we finally accept that GOD is Love, can we move to this next plane of true, divine and absolute love with GOD – Forever. This is the utmost standard of Love. *We are becoming one with GOD's Absolute Love when we die and go to Heaven. However, we can live a most loving, divine life on Earth with GOD before we die. Heaven then becomes the absolute completion of this Love!!! Pray to God very regularly. Continually ask for God's Love and assistance for yourselves and the world as a whole. That is Love!*

To add a much higher dimension of Love, which is attainable through GOD and our GOD experiences, especially considering the feelings, thoughts and experiences of Love most people enjoy, is essential for Love. It is the often expected worldly explanations and enhanced form of discovery for today's people about true Love. For many, it is a whole new approach to everyday love right through to the Absolute Love found in and through GOD both here on Earth initially, and eventually culminating at death with God in Heaven.

As people will do and believe what they choose, particularly for many in our first world countries and societies, due to them having so much and not appearing to 'need' God, it is quite possible to complete over 75 000 words, (the total number of words in this book), and not mention GOD at all, either deliberately or through ignorance when referring to love. *That must not be the case. From the book cover's title onwards, GOD'S place in any loving discussion is shown as a centrepiece of story/detail/wonderment/research on profound Love.* Note using the capitalisation of 'GOD/GOD'S' to emphasise GOD's Number One place in existence - throughout this book.

Notwithstanding, this Book 6 is the first edition - GOD is deliberately front and centre. Book 7 is the second edition of Book 6, where the author removed most references and aspects of GOD's involvement with love, to help cater for non-believers. *GOD is still included minimally. The author tries to inspire, challenge and help direct others in this position/belief to see the incredible place GOD plays in people's lives - through unquestionable Love of all equally. And how it is in everyone's best interest to devote our relationships with GOD and others to GOD.*

While we continue our search for Love and GOD, let us accept that Love is the Meaning of Life and that GOD is Love. GOD's Love gives everyone so much more than anything else can in so many senses - spiritually, emotionally and divinely, etc. It is that aspect of life that we cannot ignore and will significantly influence each of us. *As we search even further, we discover that GOD is Love and what we perceive as Love comes from GOD.* It is the highest order of influence possible for anyone, anywhere, anytime. Why? *Because not only is GOD, Love, but GOD is Absolute Love. Nothing higher exists in eternity and the universe. GOD loves humanity so much, that 'He' is permanently offering this Love to all humans, whom GOD sees as equal in all ways to each other.* Including having a capacity to sin, unlike GOD, who cannot ever sin because 'He' is Absolute Love – divine perfection cannot sin. GOD can't go against 'Himself'.

What is true love? From where does it come? How do we experience it? Is there, Absolute Love? What is Absolute Love? Is GOD necessary for me to have true love? How does GOD depth our love for each other? *What about those who don't believe in GOD, does this affect their depth of loving?*

Love is permanently coming from God to each of us. God wants us to exist forever in Heaven with 'Him'. Be open and positive to

Bryan Foster

God's loving relationship with you. That is THE LOVE we desire.

We are the ones who turn away from GOD when we sin. This is what sin is - choosing the opposite of what GOD asks and directs of us. GOD never turns away from us. Ever! We can also legitimately argue that 'He' can't turn away from 'Himself' – Love is GOD! GOD is Love! GOD can forgive everyone for sinning. It is up to us to be genuinely sorry for whatever we did wrong. To then request forgiveness from GOD and the ones we harmed/hurt. Finally, forgive ourselves fully when entirely sorry for abusing/hurting/sinning, etc.; and to make restitution to the harmed, if possible.

We are all equal creations of GOD. We are born spiritually pure. We can't sin until the age of reason, somewhere around 8-10. We can still do wrong but not understand what it is (sin) from a reasoned moral level.

Yes, we have physical blemishes and faults. But these aren't as important as our authentic selves as creations of perfection – GOD. We have the Free Will to decide to be with GOD or not. This book and its photobook companion, *Love is the Meaning of Life: GOD's Love* and *Love is the Meaning of Life Photobook Companion: GOD's Love:* assist the readers with their search for true love and GOD's place within their lives - their authentic Loving lives!

Everyone desires true love. Unfortunately, some people have enormous difficulties though because they have never truly been loved and therefore have considerable challenges relating to self and others, and GOD, in loving ways. Yet, positively, love begets love! The more love you receive, the more love you can give! And visa versa, the more Love you give, the more Love you will receive.

Hint: Start with GOD's Love of you and our Love of GOD, and the whole process becomes more straightforward. Don't sin. Try always to do your best, moving closer to GOD and each other. Appreciate GOD's massive, incredible, seniority to any other life forms. A power and force totally beyond anything we could imagine as physical humans. Divinity is so far beyond us that we must NEED GOD and then LIVE for GOD with GOD's Absolute Love's assistance.

GOD adds that extraordinary depth of love, for true love to exist entirely. We need to approach GOD continuously over our lifetimes for guidance and support. Believing this will ultimately help each person discover a Love beyond anything imagined. Believe it. Have Faith. Become one with GOD's Love.

Having that unconditional support and guidance from GOD allows our love for others and their love for us, to be otherworldly - to be at an unexpected depth of engagement. For many, it is to be in a divine relationship with GOD. How? Imagine the lifestyle and faith of any saint or religious martyr, or any legitimately holy person, etc. To be true lovers, we need to have an integral place for GOD, prayer and loving lifestyle in our everyday lives. Love is a lot more than a husband and wife's love for each other, their parents' and children's relationships, even though all these are essential. We will explore the different forms of love, which may exist in our lives, each other's and the world today.

Love is the Meaning of Life: GOD's Love is the sixth book in Bryan Foster's *'GOD Today' Series (2016-2021).* The previous five books highlighted various Revelations from the twenty-one Revelations and other numerous inspired messages GOD revealed to the author over his life so far. The Revelations occurred substantially at three significant times in his life being - 1982, 2016 and 2018. The latter two were received from GOD in the early morning hours, both around 3 am, on the plains of Mt Warning, Australia, while caravanning. On both occasions, I was directed by GOD in my minds-eye to write these down and also not to overthink what was happening.

The first book in the Series also highlighted twenty-six examples from the author's life when GOD intervened with inspired messages or directions. Love was an integral aspect of all these stories. *Sharing our genuine love stories, especially those where GOD's part is relatively straightforward, helps us understand our appreciation of love and how this love is central to our natural happiness with each other and with GOD.* We can diminish the depth of love we experience if we ignore GOD's absolute love for each one of us separately and communally. Yes, there is a high level of faith needed to receive GOD's Revelations and messages, etc. *Just as we believe certain things in our physical world without seeing these, we need to think in GOD's ways, without seeing GOD directly. God can be experienced on all levels, depending on our beliefs and love of GOD.*

The primary and essential question introduces this book: What is love? This question will be explored from both the secular (non-religious) and spiritual viewpoints. There are so many aspects, and features of love that are needed to be explored in considerable depth to gain a proper appreciation of love and how it affects us individually; how what we do, think and believe is real. These will be placed within various themes and experiences of the author and others. Each is a down-to-earth exploration and finding. Each is real and will have a different reaction according to the reader's own experiences. Even though we all can experience love and live a fully loving life, this may differ from others' appreciation and love experience. A person's background experience of love, or lack thereof, is crucial for their love of self, GOD and others.

Before this is explored, the challenges to love are discussed. In most situations, people could improve their relations with others, whether in outright loving relationships or as one of a myriad of levels of loving relationships, through to general worldly friendly relationships. Various solutions are offered to maintain our loving reality, no matter the depth to each person concerned. This Book 6 is fundamentally one person's appreciation of the existence of Love from GOD and its place in a struggling world. To then hopefully inspire and challenge the readers on their journey to Love, GOD and others. For some, hopefully, this may be their first time searching for and eventually finding GOD and/or Love. Where helpful, the previous books in this Series will be referred to, to help depth what is occurring in this book's narrative. Everyone's personal stories should help themselves build and develop their loving relationships on all levels. These successful examples of loving relationships are often becoming known to themselves and others as they try to reach a higher degree of personal love in their lives.

We next consider how GOD impacts on our relationships, whether we are aware of GOD's impact or not. Readers are invited to join this journey to appreciating GOD in loving relationships. Once again, both the challenges to this belief and various solutions to the challenges are detailed.

Love is both a most difficult concept to appreciate, as well as a most rewarding and life-enhancing strengthening of what it is to be fully and completely human. Love is integral to, and the basis for, our full humanity, relationships and relationship with GOD and all of GOD's creation. A depth of understanding and appreciation of love explains how and why love is integral and necessary for each of our lives. Love is also an aspect of the natural world of the fauna and flora. *People often feel contentment when surrounded by both pets/animals and flora. Each group's life forces are here to help each of us feel and find GOD in all of creation. That special place nearby or even our backyard becomes a place of solace and positive life-forces.* Acknowledge these and be at one with them, because this will assist you on your path to fulfilment with GOD. I have developed a relationship with four birds which occupy my backyard for most of each day – two magpies and two pigeons. Each pair has one with injuries, which inhibit most flight opportunities. They often get challenged and attacked by other birds of their species. Not only have I gained considerably from observing evolution at work, sadly in these cases, but these birds bring me a real peace through our earthly creations, fauna and flora. I believe that GOD has gifted me these animals' lives to help me grow closer to GOD through each bird. I wonder if the same would happen to each reader? I'd like to think so!

Love is the basis of life! It is the meaning of life for what we strive! It is what gives life an incredible depth. It is from the Love we know individually and in family and community etc. that each of us will need to manage all our endeavours, problem-solving and successes. Hence, those with a low quality of life-experiencing love will more than likely have difficulty, at least early on in a relationship, knowing what love is and what it can do for us. Over time, with the person developing their loving experiences, more success and appreciation of love hopefully could evolve. *Wherever we are on the love continuum, will impact on the choices we make. Love is central to these choices. It is up to each person to aim for and try to bring themselves closer to each other, but significantly closer to the Only, One, True GOD of the Universe - ever.*

Please join me on our 'love, life adventures and experiences'. Sometimes, these are unique and special, just as GOD's love for each one of us equally. People will all have experiences related to these. It is what we do with the experiences which counts

44

considerably within our lives. *Exploring how and why the only One GOD for all religions and people of all time leads us to live with GOD's absolute love, is a most freeing, exhilarating and rewarding spiritual and emotional response.*

Are we on our personal life explorations and adventures? Are we aware of when these life situations arise and could have a major impact on our lives? Are we authentically open to these experiences and life-changing adventures?

GOD is just waiting for us to say, 'Yes!' 'Yes, I can!' 'Yes, I want GOD to be a deep part of my life.' 'Yes, I want to be a deep part of GOD's existence too!' 'I love GOD, and GOD loves me, beyond anything else I could imagine.'

Once we open ourselves up to GOD and let go of the negativity or disbelief we often feel in our world today, we will eventually feel GOD inherently and close by. This will allow and encourage us to start or continue, our journey towards and with GOD. In time, with constant acknowledgement of GOD and GOD's magnificence and awesomeness, and our continuous calling on GOD to assist us with our lives, relationships and human needs, we will initially become one with GOD but in our human form.

GOD's 'Kingdom' can exist for us on Earth. A 'Kingdom' full of genuine love, forgiveness, justice, compassion, empathy, and all the other GODly characteristics we aspire to when we accept that we are now 'in the image of GOD' – not physically because GOD is divine, but spiritually. Our experience of these loving characteristics, above, then takes on a whole new depth of reality. We engage and experience GOD and all others as special and unique, even the evil ones. We need to be careful with how we engage with those existing far away from us on the positive personal characteristics' continuum, at the wrong end for loving GOD. Yet, we know that GOD desires all people to be good, helpful and loving of all others, even the bad people. 'He' is hoping that we can develop these other people on the opposing end of the love continuum to also be as loving with our almighty GOD and of each other. However, no matter whatever the attraction may be, never place yourself in danger. The approach to the evil ones mustn't be from children or adolescents. This is for willing adults who can read the situations much better than our young ones. No significant risks should ever be taken to assist others. You may need police assistance, etc., depending on the threat.

GOD is forever calling us to 'Godself'! Calling us back home to GOD! This is how our salvation with GOD in Heaven develops. Love GOD, as GOD loves each of us equally! Love each other as GOD loves each of us. Regular prayer, helping others in need and looking after ourselves and those close to us is essential for GOD! We need to be continually in contact with GOD for GOD's assistance, love, support, and directions, to name a few! Through this engagement with GOD and more and more with each other over time, we bring aspects of Heaven to Earth in some degree which is very worthwhile for us from GOD. *The more Love we spread throughout our world, the closer we become to GOD on Earth before we are in Heaven.* We can live Heaven-like experiences on Earth – by being as similar to God as we possibly can; aiming for the true love of all living creations, especially people; and asking continually for GOD'S support and guidance.

These suggestions above and our own and others' *personal experiences, all play a critical part in our positive development with GOD and humanity. GOD is always correct. GOD's instructions are always the Truth. Everything we genuinely feel right and positively about and with GOD is most likely the Truth.* However, be careful not to misinterpret everything being from GOD. *Discerning the Truth is so necessary.*

GOD and GOD's awesome goodness is our primary aim and intention for life

GOD is always correct.

GOD's instructions to us are always the Truth.

Everything we genuinely feel right and positively about and with GOD is most likely the Truth.

However, be careful not to misinterpret everything being from GOD.

Discerning the Truth is so necessary.

GOD and GOD's awesome goodness is humanity's primary aim and intention for life!

Bryan Foster

What
is
Love?

Some
Everyday
Answers

Introduction - 'What is Love?'

What is this Love we are all trying to gain and be able to share with others? GODly and divine Love is that most special relationship between people and GOD, and people and people with GOD's assistance. It is a way humanity can experience some of the heavenly qualities offered by GOD. GOD puts us all equally first with no favourites. GOD is Absolute Love! True human love is when you are prepared to put GOD first before anyone or anything else. Your other special people you Love come next. It is when you believe that you are both one - together equally in all that is Love. And that GOD comes first in everything we do, think, feel LOVE! GOD is a necessary part of any genuine appreciation of Love - being Love (as GOD is)! GOD's Love is the meaning for us living for a living! We respond to God's calling us to love.

There are various levels of love in the world today. Because this word is thrown around so much, you would be forgiven for thinking that a 'perfect' strawberry or your family pet or career is love, e.g. 'I love my job!' Let's explore some of these explanations, obviously starting with the only Absolutely Loving forever, and our personal creator – GOD!

But firstly, let us consider - the 2nd world and 3rd world situations. Suffice to say, as may be seen most times the television or other digital devices are viewed on this topic or similar: their poverty, lack of good services for hygiene, poor lifestyles and health, home quality, security, education, comfort, etc., is a real dilemma and difficulty for the 2nd world and mostly for the 3rd worlds. Surprisingly for some, many of these people are relatively happy accepting their lot in life. Yet, this is no excuse to ignore or not help them in this somewhat cruel world of the poor. Most of us in the first world never have to experience or live this lifestyle and predicament! It is challenging for this world's people to honestly and genuinely claim they can understand what the poor are going through. We, the 1st world, must take a high level of responsibility for these people's impoverished existence. Social justice, genuine love for people, and GOD, etc. demand that we are significantly fairer across our globe. Hands up those happy to share their spoils! That are happy to give up a level of most things until equality is reached. Until we can reply to these sorts of questions with, "Yes," there is minimal social justice at all across the world.

We, the 1st world countries, are failures at these times! Greed wins again. Truthfulness is also lost as it becomes hidden by the powerful and wealthy. If we are hidden from the bad Truth – we can get lost and become one of them – claiming no worries from those who have so much – let's just get on with life as we are used to doing??? STOP!!! How can we do this to others? No one is entitled to any more than anyone else. That's the hidden Truth.

Also, we can't even think that GOD won't know! GOD will know. GOD already knows what you are going to do at any time in your life. But you still need to do it, to make your own decision (whatever that is) when, where, why, how and what. You still need to make your own choices with your own Free Will. This is how it works for God. God is looking out for as much love as possible from all people in all ways. Love grows within each person as you move towards GOD in your life. Evil actions and beliefs move you away from God freely.

The highest order of love starts with GOD. The absolutely loving creator of the universe demands that our relationship with this entity is first and foremost and is the deepest of all loves. Most genuine religions have GOD as the centre of the universe, for example, to love GOD above all else in Christianity. There is only one GOD in Islam, Christianity, Judaism and Hinduism, according to their teachings. However, each religion believes in their own one GOD. A few believe that their GOD is the same as another one's GOD. Book 1 in this Series, *'1God.world: One God for All' (2016)* explores this concept in depth. In Book 1, people's experiences, scriptural quotes and religious commentaries are included for their professional and personal assistance. It also has twenty-six personal stories from the author to help us discover God in today's world through others and then through our own, personal, life experiences.

Those who have a spouse or partner who is central to their existence would have the next level of love. This is the person they would 'do anything for out of love'. Of course, this is balanced with reality. The deeper the affection for this person, the deeper the commitment and ideally the deeper the reaction from the one loved. For many people, this may even be on a similar level to the loving relationship with GOD. This is often titled AGAPE LOVE - on a plane as close as possible for humanity to experience the divine.

Children resulting from these spouses or partners are on very similar love levels as existing with the parents. The main difference is that the children are born from the parents. The love for these children is as good as the spouse/partner love without the most intimate physical relationships. Good parents would do almost anything for their children. Still, they shouldn't spoil them, which would help them grow into gifted, well-balanced and successful adults, capable of impacting the world significantly in their lifetimes.

Family love follows. The extended family unit is the most passionate and supporting love beyond the personal spouse/partner/children love. It is where the relationships are 'based' on blood. The DNA very much holds these groups together in ways not necessarily possible with ordinary friendships. Yet, things can go wrong, because we are human and we fail at times.

Friendships bear similar loving relationships but mostly on a slightly lower level. However, at times, these may be unique relationships beyond ordinary friendship. A relationship which is incredibly good and healthy. Friends forever could be a call! In general, though friendships are the next level. A place where each friend of yours helps make you the best person possible. At times, you may feel that a friendship is as strong as a partner/spouse relationship.

One of the most controversial loving relationships is with a pet and/or natural flora. Humanity seems divided as to how unique these relationships are actually. It is challenging not to see the love various pets display for their carer/owner and vice versa. Pets such as dogs and cats (but not only these two groups) would especially fit this category in most instances. The look on these animals' faces and parts of their bodies show various forms of emotions. There doesn't seem to be any substantial scientific evidence of this at this level only anecdotal evidence. Many of us would hazard a guess and feel very confident that there is love in their responses. Existing with flora often brings a more relaxed state to the people concerned. Most people would probably not acknowledge this, yet anecdotally once again, we probably have similar stories. Plants and trees have a unique relationship with these people, whereby their natural flora domain brings a mere presence, which is genuinely rewarding for them. On a personal level, I usually feel incredibly close to pets, various other animals and fauna. Just sitting with most of these creations is incredibly relaxing, as one experiences GOD's variety of creations given to us for our stewardship. We are responsible for the welfare of these living fauna and flora.

A memorable experience occurs at Crystal Castle in the hinterland behind Byron Bay. The video link below is of my wife and me reacting with various plants electronically. Music is developed through an attached synthesiser with two connection points on the plant being used – one goes in the ground, another is clipped onto a leaf. Many would dispute the truth/accuracy of this; however, you hopefully won't doubt what we did and what the plants did. Either way, it is a cause of discussion about the Truth; and what is real and what is fake.

https://www.youtube.com/watch?v=7U_z0MUo4MQ

- 'Music FROM the Plants at Crystal Castle –
    Unbelievable? But very probablyTrue?

The final level of love is for all those inanimate, lifeless objects and other emotions, which we all too easily name as love. For example, I love my pillow; I love my job. I love the holidays, etc. No one would dispute these being special, but these are not examples of love but more examples of 'like'. Love is a two-way response. There is no two-way affair occurring in these just mentioned examples. One way is not deep love, except God's love for all of creation, which we could never match on any level. God offers his LOVE to everyone equally. It is up to each of us to decide if this is what you want and should – want and NEED God.

Another commonly used example of the 'love' term is when referring to sexual passion. When this is an integral aspect one shares with their loving spouse/partner, it should take the relationship to a high level if treated genuinely and adequately. Loving passion is an integral aspect of any deep love between two adult people in a life-long commitment. However, this would be more 'lust' than love if it is purely a physical relationship devoid of the deep love just described. It is an example of how we are lustful with this other person. But it isn't the same as the emotion of love displayed in a truly loving relationship.

Let us particularly consider human love and how Forgiveness and social justice are crucial to these loving relationships. There can not be a genuinely loving relationship without some critical aspects of love being paramount – it starts with genuine Forgiveness. People need to be able to forgive others and themselves. These loving and forgiving responses to misbehaviours and other weaknesses, some being indiscretions and wrongdoings, all the way up to serious evil responses or leading evil lifestyles, justify how we make authentic love truly real. Everyone also needs to incorporate social justice within their loving relationships. They need to start with appreciating how all people are equal in the eyes of GOD and how we need to treat all people with dignity, respect and equality. The social justice enacted by all people at whatever level is required and capable of doing, allows true love to grow and flourish within themselves, their committed partners, families and communities.

What is Love?

People have various genuine thoughts, beliefs and experiences on this question.

What can we gain from others?

Those who want authentic Love, need the depth ensured when adding God as number 1 to the mix.

Communicating regularly with God adds so much to all our Loving human relationships.

Having God always on our side in anything, especially Love, is a most incredible gift from God. Believe it and experience GOD!!!

Other kinds of Loving relationships also occur without God fully involved.

These are also authentic but not as strong as would be gained from God's involvement.

I Love You

"You are the love of my life!" or "I love you!" etc.

How often have these remarkably enticing and impelling words been uttered throughout the millennia?

The utterers of such wisdom are usually referring to their spouse/partner, GOD, their parents and children. On other levels of love are the different groups we 'love' – sibling, best friend or relative, etc. Yet, we can't include everything here. Otherwise, it diminishes the true 'love' to which we refer and can most often tell the difference. For example, what level of love suits this list - Car? Smartphone? Cat? We can't love our dog anywhere near as much as we love our children. Children must be loved more than their pets. Imagine how out of skewer the world would become if pets were treated equally or better than our children or spouses or partners.

This whole notion of life-long love with people is the basis for most, if not all, of our actions throughout our lifetime. Love is the ever-calling, ever-demanding aspect of our lives. Without love, who are we?

Love is not just some philosophical discussion; it is the most inherent and integral aspect of our individual and communal lives! I dare say that without it, we cease to exist as a complete human being. A person needs to interact not only with others but with the self. This person is on the real human journey. That is the point. We need to search through ourselves and our place within our community, to find where we fit into this most loving of places, in time and space, matter and energy, and most of all in spirit.

We must not lose sight of our spiritual side. Many influences from within the western world are trying so hard to destroy this aspect of our lives. It is trying to fill this with aspects of the 'big void', materialism and self-centeredness, etc. Yes, it is often complicated to admit to this occurrence. Yes, it is often challenging to even see at times. But yes, it is so vital for our soul, or whatever you want to call that aspect of life that ties us incredibly strongly to the one and only creator GOD for all people for all time!!!

Once we accept these various forms of love and levels of love, we can genuinely grow in our love to be as close to GOD as possible. This divinely inspired growth should be our primary aim in life. One of the critical reasons for this is that the closer we are to GOD, the more robust and more realistic our love for others can be.

As we experience a unique closeness with GOD, our priorities and values change to a higher level. We can love more vigorous and more efficiently than we could ever imagine. The place of others becomes a central aspect of our lives. An intimacy develops beyond the everyday belief in love to become a much higher order of love and one where GOD's creations, on all levels, are seen in a new light which glows magnificently.

Love is the ever-calling, ever-demanding, yet absolutely necessary aspect of our lives.

…the closer we are to God the stronger and more realistic can be our love for ourselves and others.

Family Love

A loving family is the most vital unit within civilised and tribal groups alike. Family love is the most effective form of earthly love! It needs to be nurtured, supported and encouraged. Successful families could be voluntarily evaluated and modelled on, to help others without such depth of love. Otherwise, there needs to be a greater preparedness to share what works and what doesn't in mature loving relationships.

When each person truly loves the other, great things happen! Differences are accommodated, successes are celebrated, challenges are issued, respect is integral, and most importantly, Forgiveness is offered and received wholeheartedly, to name but a few actual outcomes.

A mother's love for her child. A husband's love for his wife. A daughter's love for her siblings. A son's love for his father. And the cycle goes on into an often complex and beautiful web of family relationships of love.

Family members are gifted with blood relationships. Nothing is more substantial or everlasting - except for creating a new bond between husband and wife, leading to the loving union creating children.

Out of respect for one another, individuals are encouraged to be themselves. To be the people, they desire to be. These individuals will grow as people over time - even if the direction taken is contrary to accepted family norms. At times this will lead to challenges within the family, yet a genuinely loving family should have the ability to overcome most, if not all, challenges. Or at least be able to get other friends, colleagues or relationship specialists to help.

Family members will be open to challenges issued within the family: challenges to strengthen outside relationships; challenges to improve themselves in specific or general ways; challenges to be an integral and valued member of the family.

All within the family should celebrate successes. At times this will be difficult for various members as they grapple with personal challenges, insecurities and dilemmas.

When each member celebrates another person's success, they grow personally within and beyond the family. They grow in self-worth and love for the other. Once this is discovered, the whole family unit grows and is strengthened and unified.

Being forgiven is an awe-inspiring moment for any family member, especially if the Forgiveness is because of some extreme hurt from or against another within the family.

Society needs to model successful and loving families and not just accept without challenge dysfunctional ones. Dysfunctional families are real. Some would say, the norm these days. A devoted friend, family member, or other society members needs to assist these families or encourage those struggling to improve so that each family becomes more loving within and beyond the family unit themselves.

Families are the strength of any society. The stronger the family is, the stronger the society. Society needs to encourage and support healthy, loving families and support those who are struggling.

Families are the necessary strength of any society.

The stronger the family is in Love, the stronger the society.

Society needs to encourage and support strong, loving families,

as well as to support those who are struggling and disadvantaged, who need our help...

we can not ignore the calls from the poor!

To ignore these is to not LOVE!

We are always just one moment away from death!

All of us must work, play, live and love together within our community.

Love changes all

Once someone knows and appreciates what true love is, their whole approach to life, self and others changes. Love changes all!

It is often frustrating to see the emphasis people place on being superior to others or continually trying to be better than others, all for their perceived self-gain. It is time that these people stopped thinking that because they had good fortunes and opportunities in life that they are somehow owed something special in addition to what others have received on life's journey who were not as fortunate.

They may have studied for many years. They may have spent all those extra-long hours at work: day after day, week after week, year after year - investing in the future. They may have sacrificed all those family hours for their career and a considerable income. But in all reality - so what!?

I too did once happily justify all those extra hours at university, at work and away from family. I too eventually saw reality and the realisation that the golden earthly rewards were mostly an illusion compared to what God offers freely, out of genuine and real Love.

What counts are the relationships of love. Love for self, family and all others within our world.

I realise that certain people will see these claims as a 'pie in the sky' philosophy. It certainly did for me - once.

How often do you hear from those who have stared death down

in the face or those who complete a total life-change, that all the money in the world, the most incredible job in the world, the most fantastic lifestyle in the world all mean nothing relatively compared to those loving relationships that count in that person's life - i.e. the most incredible family and friends in the world!?

Unfortunately, many people, either consciously or subconsciously, see 'friendships' as a business proposition. You cannot buy a loving family and friends. If it appears that you can 'buy' friends then, unfortunately, these are not real friends for the right reason - these are the people who usually expect to gain something from the friendship. These people see it as an investment, which will reap the rewards for them in the future.

Once you reach the happy, loving disposition, it becomes easier to add the next layers of relationships to the mix - the community in which you live, and the world in which you are an integral member.

Once I had a car, which I thought was the most remarkable feat of engineering possible (as you do?!) - and it seemed close to that level for me? After driving it for a few weeks and getting over that initial 'love-affair' with an inanimate object, I began to wish that all people could drive such a car. I did not want to be the only one with such an opportunity. I wanted to share the experience. I did not want to be so special and feel good about myself because of something I had, and others did not have. Sharing life's opportunities and rewards with others, enjoying their joy and your's, is so very special for all concerned.

Being aware of the 'istics' is part of the journey. This was when I realized that I had matured from that youth filled person years ago. That love is about sharing with others. I did not need to be so materialistic and individualist, and all those many other 'istics', which I had initially thought were the answer! Life is much simpler with the necessary needs. It is us who confuse the complexity, instead of the simplicity required with enjoyment and life fulfilments.

This is the start of an incredibly freeing experience:
• the desire to share with others
• not being someone, due to someone else not being that something
• everyone's right to have love in its most real sense in their particular circumstance - in its loving reality.

Love changes all! People need to appreciate what love truly is - people and relationships take priority. The previously mentioned 'istics' have no significance in a genuinely loving world! There are a few that do though, e.g. holistic and wholistic.

That is, holistic people, radiate that holy love that comes from GOD! This profound GODly love now experienced can significantly change us if desired and felt intimately necessary.

Once someone knows and appreciates what true love is, their whole approach to life, self and others changes.

Love changes all!

Love and Forgiveness – Essential for Love

Love and Forgiveness are both essential for True Love!!! Most people find Forgiveness the most challenging aspect of love. To forgive others and to be forgiven ourselves is quite a challenging experience! Yet, this is essential for the repairing of any loving relationship.

Once we can forgive others and forgive ourselves, we are on the way to once again exist in that reality of love - the meaning of life.

Not being able to forgive, or be forgiven, tears away at our very self. We feel less of a fully human person. We feel damaged and sometimes even irreparably so. We feel that love is less in our lives or even missing.

Some people will claim that Forgiveness is not always necessary. That time will heal all wounds. That all we need to do is to get on with our lives. I believe that on most occasions, this is just a cop-out, a search for an easy way out - yet not a real solution. (Unfortunately, some circumstances may lead to this through unexpected realities, e.g., loss, departure, or death of one party involved.) Even if most of the hurt can be forgotten with time, there is always some remnant of damage, inescapable pain, somewhere in the conscious or subconscious. This pain will invariably rise to the surface in the future, most likely when a similar circumstance prevails, as was originally the hurtful situation.

We need to offer Forgiveness if we are the perpetrator of the harm. We need to take that most challenging step to begin the process of recovery and reconciliation. When we offer

Forgiveness, the person who has been hurt has the opportunity to start the process of returning to love.

Suppose we are the ones harmed, and an offer of Forgiveness is not forthcoming from the other person or group of people. In that case, we may need to expedite the situation through diplomatically giving them the chance to begin the reconciliation process. Diplomacy is often the best method; however, a more direct approach is necessary for some people, but still needs to be done out of love, in a caring and respectful way.

When we are offered Forgiveness, we have the opportunity to begin to or be reconciled. We need to accept the offer as soon as possible and work towards repairing the relationship.

The process may be quick and clean. However, it also may take time depending on our personal history with the person involved and their personality.

We often need to forgive ourselves. This can be quite difficult. We need to learn to accept our own Forgiveness and move on, just as we do when accepting Forgiveness from others or when we offer others Forgiveness.

Forgiveness is a crucial aspect of any loving relationship. To forgive allows the relationship to return to its proper loving place. Forgiveness is divine.

Forgiveness is divine.

Love is Celebrating the Success of Others

True love enables people to celebrate the successes of others.

When people experience what love truly is, they love to celebrate everyone's successes - not for themselves but for those who have achieved. In this situation, the person who has achieved feels a sense of accomplishment, but the other feels happiness and joy.

Loving people will encourage and support others to achieve success in their lives. They will be there on their journeys, subtly offering necessary advice, etc., but always out of utmost respect for the other person. At no stage will they make the person feel inferior but will help them feel like an equal. Through this respect and subtle guidance, a genuinely loving relationship will grow and out of this, the other will feel worthy and successful.

Why is it that so many people have difficulty doing this? Is it jealousy? Is it a lack of personal self-worth? Or maybe it is a competitive streak which sees no bounds? Perhaps it is even that people don't realise that it is crucial. They may not even know that it is real and necessary?

For whatever way it is, these people are missing something extraordinary, often because of life experiences.

These people may need assistance to build their self-esteem, self-worth or an appreciation of where competitiveness begins and ends. The growth process invariably takes considerable time. After all, those who experience true love have, more than likely, developed to this stage over a substantial amount of time - often over many years.

A loving person will consider all this and accept where those people may be at any particular time in their lives' journeys. A loving person will not judge these people but will support and encourage them through the challenges they face.

Being able to celebrate others' successes is a true sign of love! Being able to do so naturally - without question and without looking for something in return - is a high point of love!

True love enables people to celebrate the successes of others...

In this situation, not only does the person who has achieved feel a sense of accomplishment and valued, but the others feels happiness and joy also.

True support. True LOVE.

Lifelong Friends are Forever (LFF)

The value of lifelong friends, particularly those formed in the early years of life, is beyond this world. Don't those special friendships begun so long ago mean so much now? Overall, the years and experiences some friendships defy the test of time. GOD has given us some exceptional people for some extraordinary reasons. Often, we aren't even aware of these reasons!

Often due to these experiences' intimate nature and the life-changing ones shared over such an extended period, these special friendships may even be on a similar level as a family. Because of this, people need to appreciate the uniqueness and specialness these allow to be shared.

Some people trap some people to treat these extra special friends with too much familiarity or even disrespect. Being very close to someone does often affect people to hurt the other person knowingly or unknowingly easily. Familiarity breeds contempt sometimes.

How often is it that the ones we love we hurt the most?

Having special friends who last a lifetime is something beyond the everyday. These are friends who would often do anything for that friendship. Never abuse this possibility. Never take advantage of these few, extra special, loving relationships.

Treasure these special friendships as these are like diamonds – rare, beautiful, unique and worth every dollar.

There also may be times needed away from each other for some energising and refreshing of the relationship. This is good and helpful. Use it wisely.

Love is Social Justice for All

'Let's be fair about this!' 'Give a mate a fair go!' 'Don't 'kick' the down and out!' 'If not for the Grace of GOD, there go I...'

How often have you heard these sorts of comments? How often have you thought about helping a friend or someone unknown to you? How often have you yearned to help someone less fortunate than yourself? I guess we are challenged by these comments or thoughts quite regularly. These thoughts are good – but what we do about the ideas is the crucial point!

How much love must it take to help an unknown, especially if friends or family challenge your actions? Why do we have an inherent desire to help others? Is it because it is universally, the right thing to do? Is because it is Godly?

I believe it takes a special love – a true love - to do this: to help someone you do not know; to help someone when your friends encourage you not to help, and to help someone who truly needs your help!

It saddens me greatly when I hear over many decades, selfish comments, such as:

'Every person for themselves!'

'It's a dog eat dog world out there!',

'The only person who counts is you!'

'Don't help them they are only using you!',

'If you don't look after yourself no-one will',

'If they were serious, they would help themselves/get a job/have a bath/etc.'.

Real love desires to help all people immensely. To significantly help your family. To help your friends. To help others who need our help. To help those who do not have what we have! All this is relative! How each of us can help, or do help, depends so much on our circumstances. That's love!

Watching television and internet shows, which display how people who have so much yet also have an inherent need to help others, react, etc. is quite compelling, along with those who have very little and regardless still do help others accordingly.

I often wonder if these individuals are more concerned with being noticed publicly through the media 'for their good works of charity' or whether they are doing the television show for altruistic reasons, and are very interested in motivating other people, particularly the rich, also to become active participants and givers for those in need. I tend to think that both sorts, and more, become involved in such shows. I also know of some very wealthy people who do not want any kind of limelight associated with such shows but wish to give considerable amounts of money and time to the needy anonymously.

We all need to commit to genuine acts of love beyond our own safe, everyday environment. Yes, looking after family and friends is very important – so is helping those in desperate need. We only need to look to those ideal models we see throughout history to see that looking after our private world is not enough! Consider

Jesus, Gandhi, Mother Theresa, and others, such as Bill and Melinda Gates and other extremely wealthy people in many ways, with or without money, as classic examples of people looking well beyond their comfort zone. Consider those people you know of, or have heard about, in your area where you live, who do so much for others. Consider how you would feel if you joined these people to assist those in need within your neighbourhood, town, and city.

My favourite charity is 'Rosies: Friends on the Streets'. This group of exceptional people, similar to many other organisations worldwide, assist those in need on the streets in major centres, in this case throughout the east coast of Australia. I have been involved with Rosies in various ways over the years, from regular nights on the streets to fundraising, and active support when challenged by the powers that be, etc.

The silent voice is an unheard cry from the needy, the poor, the ill, the lonely. These people who have so little means are not heard beyond their immediate existence by the noisy self-absorbed world. We need to show true love initially. Let us all commit to helping those in need close to where we live, as a start.

Why do descent human beings have an inherent desire to help others?

Is it because it is universally the right thing to do?

Is it GOD's love carrying us forward?

What about those who don't desire to help?

The voice of the silent is an unheard cry from the needy, the poor, the ill, the weak and the lonely...

These people who have so little means are not heard beyond their immediate existence by the noisy, self-absorbed, selfish world.

To show true love, let us all commit to helping those in need in any way we possibly can...

Let's start with those suffering and close to our own home – our families.

Love is Giving

Love is giving to others. When people love people, they provide assistance, advice, time, finance, etc. to others. When a person is genuinely in love, giving to their partner/husband/wife/ children/parents is such a natural aspect of their partnership.

When people are very much in love, they get to a stage where they want to give more than to receive. Or close to this level of giving. That is how many people get to know that the one they want to give to is that exceptional person - the person they would like to commit themselves to for their lifetime.

We then have love being shared in everyday life. People help family members, community members and groups, the sick and dying, the disadvantaged and the suffering from inadequate provisions for a healthy life. Political prisoners, corrupt unions, companies and governments, cause much angst and often resulting in unjust effects on the average citizen.

If most people on this planet decided to love their fellow humans, then equality would become more possible and real for many millions more. Our Earth has enough materials and resources to supply every person with enough to live a reasonable quality of life if we so choose to share. This shared wealth would lead to a more peaceful and loving world, as those without them gain greater equality and have fewer problems to attend to daily. It then becomes a time to love and share with humanity. Greed needs attending to for this outcome to eventuate.

Love is Giving – Especially When Catastrophes Occur

Love is Giving of ourselves and other vital aspects of our lives - this is especially shown through a lifestyle and the quality of friendship and community welfare displayed by the populations. Many countries have suffered various catastrophes requiring a large population's assistance. The level of success varies considerably around the world. One example, for simplicity, is in Australia. The coming together to help those in need and seriously affected is commonly known as mateship, as demonstrated throughout the flood covered Queensland eight years ago, or the massive fires Australia-wide in 2020. Australia is a country of extremes of climate. It is quite normal for any one year to have many extremes, e.g. droughts, floods, bush fires, often covering thousands of square kilometres. As an example, the raging bushfires of 2019 and the many droughts from 2016 to 2019, etc. Dates vary for individual places across the continent.

2020/1 saw the pandemic, COVID-19 severely affect many countries. Over four million worldwide died, and tens of millions were infected. In Australia, all states and the federal government combined to form a national parliamentary ministry to plan and implement the pandemic's various stages. The national parliamentary committee made multiple decisions, with each state government's health departments and premiers department. There were specific border closures decided by some states, while others may not have come to the same conclusion. The actual quality of decision making varied considerably, unfortunately. Most decisions were of good quality overall, though. Unfortunately, some other countries weren't as well lead or prepared for such incidents. Planning for the vaccine is still in process and hopefully, be successfully developed and dispensed early 2021.

Uncoincidentally, these occur quite often, sometimes yearly. Since the above major mentioned floods, fires and droughts, there have also been other floods, cyclones, and natural destructive events.

Catastrophes occur such as motor accidents, violent attacks, diseases and pandemics, through to such things as power outages as supplies are cut, plane or other crashes, etc.

These are just a few examples of where people give unconditionally to others during bad times anywhere world-wide. Volunteers are usually a significant number of helpers. We all have stories of other nature and catastrophes, causing severe problems and causing many sacrifices from those affected directly and indirectly.

Many examples exist worldwide, so I'll explain the significant flood already introduced, as a relevant example used to help place these 'Generous volunteers' in perspective. The first responders are the goto's when these events occur. They are also salaried, as this is their primary source of income. One absolute hero was the dad of a student I taught in year 10, who as a firefighter and rescue personnel was one of the first volunteers to be sent to the Christchurch, New Zealand's earthquake. His job was to crawl through the wreckage, often collapsed large city buildings, find those trapped and arrange for their rescue with the rest of his team. That was exceptional true LOVE for his fellow humans.

The major flood eight years ago, literally covered three-quarters of my state, Queensland, Australia, over three weeks. As a comparison, floodwaters in Queensland have covered: five times the size of Great Britain, or twice the size of Texas, or four times the area of Japan. The state capital city, Brisbane, was severely affected during that time. The CBD was shut down when power was cut for days.

Thousands of volunteers, including older school children, helped throughout Queensland, assisting those whose houses, businesses, schools etc. that had been damaged. Neighbours were freely giving time and goods to others who have been flooded. People are travelling between cities and towns to assist. The coordination of search and rescue, rebuilding infrastructure, keeping up morale and volunteers, etc., led by the state's Premier and country's Prime Minister, has been outstanding.

Even though Australia is a country of excessive natural disasters, such as floods, bush fires and droughts, etc., no-one predicted anything like this. This is by far the greatest natural disaster to hit the country for a very long time. (Covid-19 pandemic, 2020, could be considered equally or as a greater disaster over time.)

About a half of Australian mining resources are mined in Queensland, and a similar percentage of various agricultural goods are grown in this state. It will take months, if not a couple of years, for people to rebuild their houses and businesses; for the public infrastructure to be repaired or reconstructed; and for the economy to return to normal.

However, the true Australia spirit of mateship, of giving everyone a go - no matter their nationality, religion, career, wealth, etc. is prevailing - and prevailing very strongly! That's LOVE.

TRUE LOVE means giving! True love is not about taking! It is particularly in times of absolute turmoil and destruction that true love is seen as real and visible. These floods have brought out the best in people. Thousands and thousands of volunteers are currently doing just this. Good news is that very little looting or crime has occurred during this period!

The thousands of people who have been directly affected by this catastrophe have likewise been helping others in need. Flooded neighbours have helped neighbours, towns have helped towns and cities have helped cities. That's LOVE.

The recovery bill was well into the 10s of billions of dollars. Special thanks go to all the people throughout the country and world who have been generously giving financially to assist - this is love in action. Money is critical to the successful rebuilding program - for people's lives and public and private infrastructure.

Australia has been famous for its generous spirit of mateship and genuine camaraderie. People genuinely do value others, especially in their times of need during hardship and struggle. It is such a pleasure to be able to witness this in action - TRUE LOVE wins!!!

People react similarly worldwide, for all the variety of natural and 'man-made' disasters faced by humanity. When a person has empathy for others, helping others in their times of need is considered essential and the norm. They TRULY LOVE their 'neighbours'. Often these people react to a questioning person or group of the unsympathetic, with disbelief. They would answer with something like, how could you not help those in need? How could you be so selfish? If they were named as heroic for their assistance, the typical reply would be along the lines of, I am no hero, anyone would do this to help their neighbours, etc. They would add, real heroes are those firefighters, air-sea rescuers, police, ambulance and paramedics, to name but a few.

TRUE LOVE

True love means giving!

True love is not about taking!

It is particularly in times of absolute turmoil and destruction that true love is seen as

real and visible.

Love 'saves the day' for many.

We are all equal – an example

I realise this belief/statement is rejected by many. But because it is the Truth from GOD, the ramifications are enormous! It is Revelation #8 from GOD to the author on 29 May, 2016 – "We Are One". (*Where's GOD? Revelations Today*, 2018, by Bryan Foster) "All are Equal in GOD's Eyes".

As I sit here waiting for my bbq to cook at the showgrounds in Canungra, just outside the Gold Coast where I live – so much becomes very apparent – once again. This is a widespread realisation now!

Ever wonder why so many say – "Oh, I could never go camping/caravanning/RVing… I'm a 5-star person…?" Because it is in these outdoor environments that so much becomes apparent.

I sit here tonight after my dad's football team Richmond had just won the AFL grand final their first in decades and something he will never know due to his dementia. Observing those around me, camped next to me are two ladies, one whose husband went to the game in Melbourne today, along with her mother. The younger lady has a beautiful Mercedes car parked outside her mum's caravan. Across the way are two ladies and a dog, both with older cars. Over the past couple of days, both arrived independently of each other. One had a male who assisted; the other came on her own. Both are in small, quite old caravans.

Yet, amongst all these obvious differences, there is an authentic realisation that we are all equal.

There is a beautifully balanced noise of discussion and enjoyment of life happening all around me. There are many more than described above. There are numerous families with children on this last weekend camping before the school term resumes this week.

Let us all stop the pretence that we are better than anyone else.

Stop the pretence that because I have worked so hard, and maybe have taken so many risks, and succeeded, that I deserve all my gains, and others don't. That I am successful, and they aren't! Wrong! Most others have also worked extremely hard, taken risks, etc., but not 'fallen as well on their feet' as the privileged few have landed. This doesn't make them any less 'successful'. If people were honest, they would have to accept that there is so much 'luck/fortune' in people's successes. Or they have been born into wealth, nothing to do with their skills, etc. It is so much easier to start life with money than with no money! Who would disagree?

Stop pretending that any of us are better than others!

Oh yes, this does invoke numerous rather challenging outcomes. Yes, we may need to re-evaluate where we stand on this equality issue. It will challenge us to become better human beings! Yes, we will have to give more to others. No, not just to your family or good friends or professional colleagues, partners, etc.

Unfortunately, this is often far too great of a challenge for those with much. They believe they have 'earned' it all and don't need to share. We are all exactly and positively equal before GOD and therefore absolutely equal as people living with one another!

WE ARE ALL EQUAL – Once we can accept that egalitarian principle then - THAT'S TRUE LOVE

We must stop believing that we are better than others!

Share!

Genuinely believe in each other!

Assist! Love!!! Enjoy!

Humans feel the same inherently – until…!

The billionaire president of a first world country, the poor in third world countries, the sick person in a hospital, the dying, the beautiful model on a Vogue cover, the Olympic champion, our neighbour, our parent, our spouse/partner, all feel the same inherently as each other.

Human = Human.

All desire the best possible. All feel as human as each other. Everyone on this Earth feels the same intrinsically!

We all want LOVE. Happiness. Necessities. Good education. Good health. Successful occupations and careers. Successful lifestyles. Security. Freedom. Justice. Forgiveness. Etc.

It doesn't matter what we look like, our wealth, our career paths, our family, our religion, our culture, etc. we all have the same inherent human appreciation of who we are as a person.

That is until so many unforgiving forces tell us differently – i.e. along comes the 'real' world! By the way, this 'real world' is not necessarily how people claim it to be.

Various things change for everyone. We suddenly get affected by so many destructive views that we lose our genuine appreciation of who we are. We may no longer appreciate much about our true selves and others.

The media and various social platforms are echoing or creating so much societal negativity. The 'screaming' consumeristic devotees, along with the inherent doubt and vulnerability of the human entity, are often the worst instigators changing our self-perception and hence how we feel about ourselves on any given day.

The internet trolls who aim to harm others are evil at heart. This is not something people are born with; it develops in individuals most likely resulting from considerable negative experiences in their lives. These days more than ever, possible mental health issues.

Over time and with wisdom and experience, and heaps of decent people, friends and family, we hope to discover our true selves once again. Our LOVING, generous true selves come forward!

GOD wants us to feel and be truly loving, healthy, beautiful, appreciated, successful individuals, no matter our varying cultures, religions and circumstances.

We must never forget that we are equal in GOD's eyes and that GOD is always there to assist every one of us. All we have to do is ask! Ask, as we should do very regularly, as we all NEED GOD so much! Why? Because we are not divine, but human creations from the blessed, perfect and absolutely LOVING GOD.

Be prepared for the unexpected when praying with GOD. Be open to various solutions and support from GOD, with some options not being expected by you. Trust in GOD and GOD's ways. Listen in your heart of hearts for that exceptional communication with GOD. That special message or feeling. That solution to help you through the tough times when GOD will be carrying you.

Be prepared for the unexpected when praying
with God...

Trust in God and God's ways.

Listen in your heart of hearts for that exceptional
moment of communication with GOD.

That special message or feeling.

That solution to help you through the tough
times when GOD will be carrying you.

Humans, animals and plants all have a 'soul' - with a relationship with GOD and each other - as discerned by author.

This article's title above must seem like quite a strange statement to make. It should challenge most of us and lead to some extraordinary claims about life and equality on Earth. Reaching out to GOD for LOVE, assistance and compassion, etc. is critical.

The discerned claim from God to the author is that GOD made everything within this universe. For us to claim that all living things have an association with each other and with GOD is remarkable and lifegiving. The 'SOUL' is a unifying characteristic. It is LIFE for ALL those living GOD creations!

The more we experience all forms of life on this Earth from the plants on the plains to the rainforest and oceans, etc., to the animals domestic and wild throughout our world, and include humans, the highest order of life, we can create and live in a genuinely LOVING world with which we surround ourselves with GOD and GOD's creations.

Suppose we deliberately don't surround ourselves with God's creations and don't try to include many life forms of all sorts from God, as we possibly can in our lives within reason? In that case, through our beliefs and actions, we exist in a relatively pointless existence and often find a world lacking in love, support and genuine divine reality, i.e. GOD. GOD needs the best from each of us. GOD needs us all working together to help make our existence on this earth meaningful and fulfilling.

Every person needs as much of GOD as is humanly possible. GOD's creations vary considerably, yet each is important to GOD and should be for us also. There are millions of living species, past, present and future beyond humanity, which GOD desires for us to benefit from and exist with entirely.

As I sit on my back veranda and observe all flora and fauna in action, especially the birds of many species, along with the natural flora of my home region, I totally believe in GOD's place amongst all these living flora and fauna! They stand out as life itself - outstanding creations. This is an extraordinary reality. GOD is not only present in our existence and life. Many other life levels also exist in ways often unknown to people who aren't open to GOD's presence and place within both the animal and plant world!

All life-forms may even be given the option to go to Heaven or Hell! (This aspect for flora (plants), hasn't been fully discerned from God for me yet, but I strongly feel it may well soon be the case?) An adventure to Crystal Castle outside Byron Bay in Australia helped with our appreciation of plants reacting to human touch. Have a view of the video listed below. The video suggests that the 'electronics/electric charges' within plants can be read and changed into other sounds with synthesises – in this case, music for these plants. Some fairly convincing examples are shown. What do you think?

Electronically Synthesised Music from the Plants at Crystal Castle, near Byron Bay, NSW, Australia see:

https://www.youtube.com/watch?v=7U_z0MUo4MQ

The gifted, talented and fortunate OWE the world!

To be fully human, our gifts, talents and fortune must be shared within and without our societies. Sharing raises the levels of happiness for all. The greater the gift, talent, wealth, beauty, etc., the more significant the sharing demanded of all those people! The responsibility to assist others must be very high for them.

Never forget, we are all equal in GOD's eyes, and hence the need to LOVINGLY assist and raise the quality of others' lives to being equal in the world's eyes is called for by GOD. Social justice is the cornerstone for this equality.

To be free, each person needs to be an active, positive, sharing, respected member of society.

Those who choose to hide away and bury their gifts, talents and fortunes, will never be truly content or happy. They will often fear to lose what they have and concentrate on retaining or increasing this. This egotistical and selfish approach often leads to despair.

The good in all people is crying out to be freed. It is for selfish, negative reasons that people don't release the good. The fear of having nothing or having less, of losing the gifts, talents and fortune, is an extraordinarily robust and negative motivator for the ego and vulnerability fact within the human entity.

It is everyone's role to improve the quality of those who are suffering, poor and disadvantaged. Whatever gifts, talents and riches we have, we need to share these with others in a constructive, community-building way. We must use our God-given talents/gifts/riches, etc. to improve the world and those who live within it. Greed and selfishness are the main destroyers.

Have a Heart

My whole appreciation of life, literally changed, having watched the ABC (Australia) 'Catalyst' episode, 'Heartbeat: The Miracle Inside You'. A show with absolutely awe-inspiring messages, vision and simple explanations. (The internet link for the show follows this article.) Now this is truly LOVE!

An Australian heart surgeon, Dr Nikki Stamp, is brilliant as she takes us on a genuinely lifesaving journey. This is so relevant for all those with hearts! (Bit of humour there, I hope. I get this way when overtaken by brilliant medical science – especially info., which helps save lives!) Those with heart issues, or with the capacity for or physical flaws of the heart, have heart issues. (No matter your age and lifestyle, you may not even know you have problems!?)

Indirectly, it also shows the awesomeness of creation of the human heart! Some of the statistics will blow you away.

For those open to the real miracle of life, you cannot help but see the place of GOD in all this.

As iconic Australian presenter Molly Meldrum used to say in general on the musical TV show 'Countdown' – "Do yourself a[n absolute] favour! - And watch it if you haven't!"

Watch, ABC Catalyst show – 'Heartbeat: The Miracle Inside You'.

Dr Nikki Stamp explores the world of our hearts. She explores their operation, what we need to do to take care of our hearts, and explains the latest science used in surgery to repair damaged hearts. (ABC)

(http://iview.abc.net.au/programs/catalyst/SC1602H005S00)

LOVE in Nature (e.g. Oceanic Dolphins)

LOVE can be experienced through the natural world experience of LOVE - GOD is in nature. GOD/LOVE is the absolute creator of life and can be especially experienced in our natural environment.

Swimming, or observing up closely, wild dolphins and whales, brings out something quite remarkable in us. The 'Tears from GOD' experienced simultaneously through these encounters marked these experiences as incredibly memorable and life-changing for me. I have been very fortunate to have had two up close and personal experiences with dolphins. One was a dolphin purposing just a couple of meters in front of my surf ski ride, as I surfed across a wave. Another was two dolphins swimming upside down and around my daughter and me just off the beach in waist-deep water.

LOVE is there in nature but outside our typical day to day lives for all to experience and engage.

We must be open to it, yet need to be in a real loving state to engage fully with it. There are so many ways to experience LOVE

The twelve most common ways to experience genuine LOVE, I believe and have discerned, are through:

- GOD - Initially to ultimately
- Spouse, children and family
- relationships
- best mates
- our spirituality

- nature lifeforms
- pure and positive leisure and activity time
- creating things
- sharing deeply
- giving to others
- life's freely chosen vocations
- music and song

However, due to unchallenged reality, GOD is so superior to us all - totally. No ifs or buts, that's just the way it is. From God's Absolute LOVE develops all levels of LOVE experienced by us as people. God creates opportunities for all forms of LOVE; God sets these; God supports this LOVE. Just ask God for help to be LOVING. Be prepared to Give and also to take what is genuinely and LOVINGLY offered to you.

An incredibly personal experience of surfing with the dolphins in the wild of the ocean was one of the most majestic experiences of love in nature that I have experienced. It occurred at Broken Head, near Byron Bay, on the northern New South Wales, Australia.

I have experienced this twice. The other was just over a decade ago, and I was with my relatively young daughter – when two dolphins circled us while they were catching fish within a massive school of baitfish just near us, and we were swimming in the sea about waist depth for me. Each one circled us upside down twice, as they do during fishing to not be seen too easily by their hunted prey. And ended with one usual, upright circle, the right way up. This was to the point of experiencing something beyond our earthly existence. Tears flowed, along with the 'OMG', 'Oh My GOD' feeling in its most real, spiritual and genuine sense, as these dolphins circled us, one sunny, summer morning at Kingscliff, NSW, Australia.

My first experience of dolphins, up close and personal, and away from the local dolphin tourist attraction, was while I was surfing on my short surf ski at Broken Head, near Byron Bay, Australia. Byron Bay is an eclectic beachside township, primarily a holiday and wealthy beach lifestyle destination, especially for backpackers worldwide. It has a strong, diverse spiritual undercurrent and welcomes various people from the extremely rich to the old-style backpacker/hippy. It is also a world-renowned backpackers' haven - quite a fitting place to experience what turned out to be a most spiritual occurrence.

This was to the point of experiencing something beyond. Tears from God poured out while riding the crest of a wave on my short surf ski a couple of decades ago. This creation of nature, a dolphin, and I extraordinarily met that day. The cosmos seemed so small. We were ONE at that moment in time! It appeared to LOVINGLY lead me along the rather large wave, porposing a couple of metres in front of me. I did everything to remain in this moment, even though both tears and fast spraying water made seeing quite tricky. God was in, and with this dolphin and me.

On that day, I was surfing amongst some extremely beautifully formed, turquoise waves, with many schools of dolphins porpoising through, over and under the waves. On one giant wave, I was speeding across its front wall of water and had water spraying into my face at such a speed that I had to keep blinking my eyes to avoid the spray obscuring my vision. I had just come out of the tube/barrel of a wave when a shadowy black figure slid through the face of this wave's wall of water to my right and went downwards underwater in front of me. At this stage, my greatest fear was that it was a shark and all the horrible thoughts of such a situation flew through my imagination! Panic set in to such an extent that I feared to fall off the ski - but knew I had to fight to stay on, no matter what!

At that moment the shadowy figure quickly rose to the surface immediately in front of me, at about two metres, and porpoised up and down - virtually leading the way! I followed, mesmerised by what was occurring in front of me - I now dreaded to fall off out of absolute awe of this most enjoyable dolphin experience! And miss all the exhilaration which was forthcoming.

Tears and water filled my eyes - and blurred my vision! I was indeed in the most LOVING zone! I was one with nature - with a most remarkable, intelligent mammal, this wild but gentle dolphin – both of us seemed to be enjoying each other at that one moment in time on a shared wave. I subconsciously fought to maintain my balance as I was distracted and in quite a euphoric state. This dolphin, a most remarkable creation of nature with high intelligence, and me, exceptionally met that day. The cosmos seemed so small. We were ONE at that moment in time!

The literal, physical sign of divine LOVE given to us by God, 'Tears from GOD', permeated these two most beautiful, awe-inspiring experiences. LOVE in nature is real. It is also part of the meaning of life. LOVE is experienced within and outside the natural world in so many all-encompassing and enfolding ways.

Many of us have stories like these which have left a remarkable memory and experience of nature and God. Mine was in the ocean, but others will also be the ocean or anywhere else that the soul exists, maybe as well.

Throughout our lives and our world, LOVE is there for us all. We must be open to receiving and giving it. Yet we need to allow ourselves to be LOVING to experience it properly. We close ourselves off from it when we desire not to harm instead, to others and ourselves. We also have LOVE closed off from us when others psychologically or physically hurt us. Damage to self and others may be in so many ways, including the physical, emotional, sociological, psychological and physiological, etc. We need to have the courage and wisdom to go from beyond the harmful into the loving!

Live a LOVING life and LOVE will truly be
there within you and

with those you impact upon.

I was one with nature - with a most remarkable,

intelligent mammal -

this wild but gentle, safe dolphin.

Both of us enjoying each other

at that one moment in time in our shared wave.

Forgiveness of others and ourselves is often needed.

Live a **LOVING** life, and true **LOVE** will be there for you from **GOD!!!**

LOVE is so real.

LOVE is the basis of life and love is from **GOD!**

LOVE is the Meaning of Life.

Bushland Spirituality Aids Love

Nothing beats the bushland (nature) for spiritual balance and personal equilibrium. We all should have at least one place where we can feel at home spiritually - be this in the natural environment or some human-made (holy) facility for us.

It is through this that we can improve our loving relationships. Quiet, reflective time is necessary for a balanced approach to love and life.

We are very fortunate to have a few places, which fulfil this need. Mine are mostly in Australia and Canada. The two places where my children live.

Australia's craggy features, uneven but robust gums, upright and strong Australian grass trees – whether lush or burnt, golden red sunsets, eagles, dolphins, etc. etc. etc. and especially the resilience of everything standing and beneath – inspire and refresh!

My 'birthplace' of North Stradbroke Island (Straddie) is these and so much more! Is your birthplace special for you? If not, what is your place?

These past few years, I have been extremely fortunate to have spent a week or two each year on Straddie (Island), North Stradbroke Island in Moreton Bay off Brisbane. Spending time there is so refreshing, life developing and personally becoming one with the Earth and all things natural.

Driving along the long white sandy beaches and sand tracks in a 4x4 RV, watching the brilliant nighttime sunsets, walking the trails and gorges, watching the whales, dolphins and other exotic marine life on high and at close range, relaxes the mind and 'soul'.

Staying close to nature in camping grounds adds another whole new depth to these experiences. These days, camping grounds cover people's options at various stages of their lives, from tent camping through to large motorhomes, fifth wheelers, buses, and eco-cabins.

Canada's magnificent Canadian Rocky Mountains regions' rivers and creeks certainly bring nature to all those who access it. Similar to other countries with significant mountain ranges and snow-capped mountain peaks.

These are genuinely natural and beautiful experiences in all that is our oneness with the spectacular natural environment!

GOD is so present in these regions and geographic features. The natural magnificence from streams to the mountains is 'loaded' with 'Wow' moments repeatedly. It 'seems' that every corner on every road into the Rockies holds another 'WOW' moment

All this comes about through the lifeforce each human, animal and plant possess. We sense inherently, this very close association with other GOD created lifeforms. We enjoy their presence with us. Even the wild attacking types attract us, but preferably behind a caged enclosure.

Nothing beats the bushland for spiritual balance and personal equilibrium.

We all should have at least one bushland/watercourse place where we can go and feel 'at home' spiritually…

All this comes about through the lifeforce each human, animal and plant possess.

Absolute LOVE of GOD

Introduction to **GOD** is Absolute **LOVE**

The challenge for many people is in accepting that GOD is real and that GOD is LOVE. The LOVE we are all searching for and wanting it to be central to our human needs is for GOD to be an active part of our lives. After all, GOD is ABSOLUTE LOVE.

Yes, we can personally have a deep relationship with another person without GOD being present, or so we believe? However, this relationship falls short of the one with GOD being integral to our most profound connections. Logically, we must admit that being near or with GOD is being near ABSOLUTE LOVE. LOVE is one of the MOST POWERFUL genuine and authentic FORCES in this universe. Aim for GOD is an aim for Massive LOVING experiences.

If GOD is absolute LOVE, we need GOD to have a genuine role in our LOVING lives. I will argue that from my experience, GOD is real. GOD is the absolute LOVE that we need. GOD as an integral and essential part of our LOVE!

What if we don't believe in GOD or GOD's place within our LOVING relationships? This is quite possible within our ever-growing secular society. In the western world, where divorce is almost 50%, it is quite possible that GOD is not seen as an essential part of our lives, or existing within our world? Would this statistic be this high if GOD was seen as very important within these LOVING relationships? I would argue an emphatic, "No". Our challenge is to be open to GOD and GOD's role in our LOVING relationships. Even if being a non-believer in GOD or GOD's influence within our world, this is an essential aspect of being human. This is the GOD-given Free Will choice to be for or against GOD.

When times get tough, God 'carries you' - if this is what you authentically choose – you no longer need to walk on your own! Be continually open to finding, accepting and then becoming as close as possible to GOD on Earth, so that your natural inclination at your death, when asked by GOD of your final choice, is to go to GOD in Heaven. The option applies to believers and non-believers alike.

GOD IS ABSOLUTE LOVE.

We need GOD to have a genuine, authentic role in OUR LOVING lives.

It is up to us to decide the answer of the big questions! Ask GOD for help with this decision making!

Nothing is forced by GOD!

GOD is Absolute Love

GOD is ABSOLUTE LOVE. From this, GOD gives us all total freedom - Free Will - to decide to go along with GOD or not! To help others out, or not. To be open to everything GOD has to offer each of us individually, or not.

Too many people today cop out and blame GOD for anything and everything wrong in this world. Unfortunately, most things wrong have been done by humans and their free choices. Wars, violence, abuse, non-sharing of the worldly wealth but causing poverty, various illnesses related from human lifestyle choices, e.g. resulting from poorly chosen diets, smoking, alcohol and different illegal drugs, etc., lack of fitness, unsafe places and circumstances in which people choose to live, etc., have a massive impact on us all.

There is also a dimension of mystery in all of this, e.g. why did the child die so young? Why did the tsunami hit a coastline 1000s of kilometres from the epicentre and kill so many?

Because GOD is not of our physical world and is not physical but is divine and GODly, we can not imagine with any real certainty, why GOD allowed for some severe natural events to occur?

When we accept that many people claim to have gained from some form of suffering or loss, there is some clue. That their lives have been enhanced, etc. We know that out of GOD's absolute Love and our own Free Will and our Informed Conscience, GOD allows people to make their bad personal choices with the various ramifications resulting. GOD's absolute love makes this reaction necessary. The answer awaits us through our Salvation with GOD in Heaven.

GOD loves us all equally, no matter our circumstances. Imagine our world if we all similarly loved GOD and each other.

We NEED GOD!!!

Until we can say, believe and live this belief, we are nothing! We are limited to this world and all its imperfections, especially its 'holdbacks'! The world is 'soooo' very good at holding people back from everything that is their true destiny. Their ultimate self-worth, their ultimate possibilities, their ultimate realities – WITH GOD!

We are still of this world and for this world - until we leap. Until we truly believe and know we must go beyond our natural, human, every day understood capacities.

To go beyond this world, to a higher existence, while still living in this world, we have no option other than to NEED GOD! Need GOD in its most real sense. Yes, NEED GOD.

This is much greater than needing a parent, a spouse, an education, a job, money, a career or a friend. Much more significant than needing physical and emotional securities. Much greater than having all those expected and inherent, yet often withheld, human rights, social justices and freedoms.

Once we accept the need for GOD, we progress towards GOD. We can finally become one with GOD while still living our lives on this Earth. The need is one of understanding and appreciating who GOD is, what GOD is for us individually and communally, and ultimately needing GOD to lead, guide and be with us on all levels throughout our lives. Praying to God is essential for Love.

We all need to freely accept the reality of GOD, the awesomeness of the ultimate LOVING GOD, and the need to have GOD with us intrinsically and absolutely in our journey towards GOD throughout our lives. We need GOD! GOD needs us - out of Love! We have the freedom to decide on God.

Bryan Foster

Experiencing GOD Directly

GOD is Love. Love is the meaning of life. GOD is the meaning of life. My most euphoric experience of GOD started in tears of absolute Love (Tears from God) back in my 20s. It has only deepened since. I discovered early on that God only wanted the best for each of us. The rules from God, which some people dislike because these apparently 'take the fun out of life' are only negative for those who want to do wrong and evil, knowing it is so. Why would people freely choose evil and wrong?

In my mid-20s, I was extremely fortunate to experience true Love from GOD. I am an everyday Catholic. At that stage, I was a typical 20 something with all the challenges and difficulties this age group faced. The experience of Love and GOD I had was quite exceptional. Over the decades, I have now developed a fuller appreciation of what love truly is.

To truly experience, Love is to experience GOD truly. When that euphoric experience of true Love becomes real, GOD is present at the moment! GOD's meaning enters the world of the present.

The recipient becomes one with GOD, one with Love - ONE. We truly become ONE with GOD and the universe.

Tears flow in a state of euphoria! Uncontrolled and overawing. A reaction to the experience and yet one within and throughout the experience.

Once this true Love becomes one with the recipient, there is no turning back and no turning away from what is now the most essential and integral oneness with the all-encompassing loving

GOD.

Reality is now on a most intimate level with LOVE. Truth is in Love with the all-encompassing and wondrous Love of the one GOD. Love is the only direction open. The other person becomes as important as the self. Shared wisdom now must be shared with the other. The couple is unified as ONE with GOD!

The earthly world and all within take on a most remarkable metamorphosis for the renewed 'one' person. The one, GOD, now lives with and through all present - not separated from, but intrinsically intertwined with, all that coexists — no separation from the world but totally and absolutely one with all of creation and creator.

A level of existence, which is most difficult to explain, yet so simple in lifestyle. To now give so much through a genuine love of humanity, environment, and GOD without question, but purely because it is the actual existence, the previous lifestyle seems so far removed from reality. The new lifestyle is a simple one of loving the other as much as loving yourself - with GOD's help.

The new lifestyle is a simple one of loving the other as much as loving yourself.

With God's help this loving of the other is made easy - because it is so natural to do.

So right to do. So important to do!

I Love Life!!! I so much Love this Life!

I can only imagine, to a limited degree, what the next existence after death can possibly be like?

What could existing with the One and Only ABSOLUTE LOVE – GOD - Be like??? Apart from ABSOLUTELY LOVING and BRILLIANT.

What could evil possibly do to ruin our lives? Much - if it was fully known!!!!! We must be fully aware of evil's existence and solution.

GODness

How good is this earthly life? Even with all the problems, abuse, terrorism, wars, starvation, poor health, domestic violence, etc., for most people, life is extra special. For those caught up in these conflicts worldwide, life itself is so. And so necessary to be looked after, as much as humanly possible.

Evilness

For those caught up in an evil existence beyond your control, GOD is there to save you. And to save the evil ones, if they are willing to be lovers and not haters. Often this means that GOD can do something to help you along. On other occasions, you genuinely suffer, with or without GOD.

Humans make their own decisions in most cases. Some are the greedy, evil ones trying to gain something from the good people of this world. And have no caring for how much suffering these innocent people experience!

The first world countries and communities are called upon by GOD to share their values, happiness, Love, Forgiveness and wealth.

I So Love GOD!

I so love GOD!

I so love all of GOD's creations!!! - Everything with, or without, a life of its own.

Of all these, so many living creations, creatures, and flora alike MUST HAVE A SOUL. Due to having a life! (Discerned from GOD.) These souls bring everything with life together as one.

I love the way GOD loves us so much and leaves all the choices, big and small, to each of us to decide personally – through Free Will and our Informed Conscience. Yet, everyone is asked to follow GOD's teachings.

I so love the ABSOLUTE ALMIGHTY who is so beyond each of us and all of us, yet came to Earth AS THE INCARNATE GOD to spread GOD's Word about the best lifestyle we should lead while on Earth, to be One with GOD in Heaven after our deaths.

To acknowledge GOD as the ABSOLUTE ALMIGHTY, WHO HAS EXISTED FOREVER AND WHO WILL EXIST FOREVER, is incredibly sobering. This is not what many people would imagine! But it is so!!!

Most people have significant difficulties understanding and appreciating GOD at any level of existence. To then place so much on the belief in the divine GOD is beyond too many people.

Yet, be open to God's presence and desire to help us all, always! Listen very carefully! Have a special quiet place for this!

The world as a whole must begin what is needed to bow down before this Majestic Divinity. We are not equal with GOD!!! Our personal beliefs do not change the incredible reality of GOD!!! It is only we who are fooling ourselves if we think otherwise.

The LOVE GOD offers is awesome. It seems so welcoming and wholesome. It appears to help us as minute creatures with souls to accept our place on this Earth and work towards Oneness with, and for, GOD!!! No matter what we think, we are relatively so insignificant with GOD, that we obviously must follow GOD's Love and directions forever. We can't pretend or believe we are equal with God. But we are equal to all other humans throughout history and into the future – forever.

In this series, the previous textbook, Book 5, challenges one essential belief held by the two most popular world religions, Christianity and Islam. This will challenge all believers of God to justify their firmly held beliefs or otherwise change to this new Revelation explained and introduced in Book 5 of this '*GOD Today*' Series... *Jesus and Mahomad are God*'.

I have discerned from GOD over many decades that...so many living creations, creatures and flora alike must have a soul.

These souls bring everything with life together as one.

GOD is Life. God is Love. God is fully with us throughout our Lives.

GOD is ONE with US ALL.

Thank You, GOD!!!

Thank you for your fantastic GENEROSITY and LOVE which you have shown and shared with humanity and other living creations.

An ABSOLUTE PURE LOVE to be shared with all creations.

Who can't believe that at least our pets and wild animals have a living soul?

Who can't see the domestic animals with emotions and lives of their own?

The closer people become with you, the more these critical moments of Love are experienced or observed.

When individual people and humanity as a whole want to become One with You, Life starts to become So Real! Real and so GOOD!

People can start to appreciate what your Kingdom means, both here now and after death.

Their understanding of you and your desires for them become intrinsic with their lives, individually and communally.

The One and Only GOD of the universe. The only GOD to ever exist calls us all to 'Him'.

If we could only appreciate what this means, then life would make so much more sense and the desire to work with GOD in LOVE for everyone, before, now and forever would be a fundamental belief and lifestyle.

GOD makes Life so much Better!

Anybody who accuses GOD of taking the fun out of life must be joking – 'talk about 'kidding' themselves'. Life was given to them by God – some need to show respect, acceptance and acknowledge God's superiority to everything. If personal greed, lack of truthfulness and Forgiveness, etc. get in the way of knowing God – 'lose' these and move entirely over to the massive LOVE of GOD!

For those whose idea of having fun is against GOD's teachings are very ignorant of reality. If this means that people harm, hurt, destroy others, slander, etc., they are evil people.

Anyone who is regularly greedy, self-centred, thoughtless, abusive, right through to down-right evil, show their ignorance of the GODness's reality – GOD-ABSOLUTE LOVE.

When GOD teaches us anything, it is done out of Absolute Love for each human equally. It is done to assist, not impede, our's and all living creatures' or flora's quality of life.

People who ignore this for any reason from greediness to total ignorance/evil, etc. actually impede or even stop the enjoyment GOD wishes for all, especially for those associated with the negatives for whom you are acting wrongly with or for.

All of the evil or wrongdoing was done by various people to gain them more or considerably much more than the others of life's gifts - no sharing or only a little sharing here.

GOD does not do anything wrong! No matter how hard we try to implicate GOD in pain and hurt suffered by many, we cannot make this stick. GOD is perfect; we are flawed. Most of these pains and hurts, physically, emotionally, socially, healthwise, etc., are brought about by human actions to gain various groups of people more than others - considerably more on numerous occasions.

The most challenging question of all may be, why does GOD do/allow the natural world's events which harm people? That is hurricanes, cyclones, tornadoes, volcanoes, earthquakes, tsunamis, etc. Unfortunately, there is no simple answer, other than to say that often these occur as a product of GOD's creation, i.e. the universe. For example, if a significant earthquake occurred in California, most people would not be too surprised. To build on or near known faultlines, it is knowingly accepting a possible catastrophe could occur. GOD expects humans to make the right decisions, not the hazardous ones, which could cause significant deaths and injuries. The Earth is slightly shrinking, as it cools overall. Hence earth movements occur and become natural disasters.

Also, because GOD is divine and perfect, and we are human and flawed, we cannot correctly appreciate GOD's reasons for our suffering. Is it a means for us to turn to God for assistance and absolute Love? Is it to bring God much more into our daily lives? Is it showing how we honestly need God to assist when needed? We just have to trust in GOD for our betterment and loving existence. In many cases, we will not get a proper understanding of why, until we are once again with GOD after our deaths. No-matter-what, God desires the best for everyone.

We must accept what happens to or with us if we make the wrong decision.

The mystery continues as we try to come to terms with the desire for our fully human lives on Earth, along with going to Heaven with God. We don't know the hour of our death on Earth. Why do we seem to ignore the reality of dying and going to Heaven? God doesn't want us to just hang around the Earth, but to die at God's chosen time eventually, and move into our next life – hopefully in Heaven. However, it will end up in Hell for some people - the evil, hate-filled, rejectors of God.

If there is no decision to make about why it happened, e.g. a surprise serious illness, we need to turn this over to GOD and the health professionals to do what GOD desires or requires of them. The community's response needs God's support and guidance.

Once we accept God's real goodness and holiness, we can work with God on so much. We can help make each person's life so much more - so much better. God's Love for us is immeasurable. Take full advantage of this Love. Pray. Listen. Do.

Pray to God

Listen to God

Do what God says

Enjoy GOD!

GOD
and
Prayer

Prayer – Communicating with GOD

It is from and with GOD that we genuinely experience Love. To share a genuine depth of Love with other people, we need GOD to be an integral part of this. GOD is Divine and Absolute Love! We need GOD through this highest level of Love. It is achieved through our prayer and the prayerful, Godly lifestyle we live.

It is the same as those religions that celebrate marriage as a holy partnership between three - husband, wife and GOD. GOD is a necessarily integrated aspect of the height of Love for a human with another human in the state of marriage. Believing this will enable God to become real and authentic to the partnership. God needs to be invited and then communicated with, fully.

Prayer is us deliberately communicating with GOD and GOD with us. There are so many styles of prayer and worship. Each of us has to explore which forms suit us in our lifestyle, the best. Through prayer and worship, we truly become aware of our humanity, with all its faults and freely chosen flaws (Free Will), combined with times of extreme happiness, joy, and fulfilment. With GOD's help, we can depth our relationships in ways unbeknown without GOD's assistance. True Love requires us to seek out GOD's help, just as much, if not more, than our Love with our spouses, partners, children, relatives, friends colleagues and all other community members we engage within our lives.

We can come to GOD through many forms of prayers. GOD can come to us whenever and however GOD desires. Research various forms of prayer, worshipping God skills, etc.

To begin solemn prayer, we have to acknowledge GOD's prominent place within existence initially. Even though we are the highest order/species with superior intelligence and emotion, etc.

within creation, GOD is so much more – GOD is massively AWESOME, beyond any level we can imagine as a physical human being. God wants the best for each of us. GOD created us and all the cosmos. How overwhelming must GOD be?

Most of us learn about prayer through our parents, family, and religious schools and communities. Many come to GOD in unexpected ways. However, it may occur for each one of us; it is our duty to bring GOD to the centre of our lives and our world. Nothing is more significant or equivalent to GOD, the one and only GOD for all religions, for all times and forever!

Very unfortunately, others doubt or don't believe in GOD at all. GOD is forever waiting for each unbeliever and doubter of these groups of people to turn around and see the magnificence of GOD patiently waiting for each person to believe in GOD.

GOD loves absolutely and leaves the door open for the rejectors of GOD to see the light and come into the world of GOD awaiting them.

As an example of the effects of prayer happening in a somewhat different way to my everyday experience, I would like to share my Saudi Arabian visit story. It has two aspects to it, with the second one being what the Islamic effect of their call to prayer had on me. Being in Saudi Arabia during Ramadan, was the most challenging but rewarding spiritual/religious experience for me. I grew so much through this.

Be open to the unknown when exploring different prayer styles. Begin your prayer, acknowledging GOD being the number ONE of eternity and the universe. Truthfully ask God for Forgiveness for your wrongdoings. Forgive yourself as well. Then continue with whatever prayer format you are using that time.

It is from and with God that we truly experience love.

For us to experience a genuine depth of love with other people, we need God to be an integral part of this.

God is Divine and Absolute Love!

We need God through this highest level of love.

This is achieved through our prayer and the prayerful lifestyle we live.

Be open to the unknown when exploring different prayer styles.

Begin your prayer, acknowledging GOD being the number ONE of eternity and the universe.

Truthfully ask God for forgiveness for your wrongdoings. Name these if you can.

Forgive yourself as well.

Then continue with whatever prayer format you are using that time.

Saudi Arabia – Experience of GOD and Prayer Through Islam

Home of Mecca. Birthplace of Muhammad (Mahomad*). Home of Ramadan and the Hajj.

There are two parallel stories here; one is the business trip with my father; the other is Islam's impact on me due to experiencing Saudi Arabia, personally, during Ramadan.

A. Business

I was very fortunate in 1987 to visit Saudi Arabia with my dad while on a business trip. This was very different from the norm, as most people couldn't get access to this country. Because of our business association with this country, we were there to check a mining plant out. My father was evaluating its success.

We had to have been invited by one of the princes before entering. Our trip was based on Dad's special designed rock salt dredge. These dredges were primarily used for mineral sands mining. Still, for the Saudis, the dredge was adapted to suit rock salt lakes, no mean feat and an invention which became quite inspiring to many other countries and businesses. Back then, the Saudis needed their rock salt mined, and dad's designed dredge was hugely successful. Our visit was to check how it was operating, it having been built in Australia and shipped to Saudi Arabia a couple of years beforehand. Dad examined the dredge and mining plant and gave the operation a clean bill of health report.

Before entering Saudi Arabia, a mostly desert country, we had to get our passports stamped in Bahrein before crossing the 25km bridge into Saudi Arabia. A Saudi driver drove us to El Jabail where we stayed and which was close to the dredge.

B. Spiritual/Religious

The most remarkable spiritual experience for me was being awoken before sunrise with the first call to prayer for that day over PA systems throughout the country. We were in the Islamic month of Ramadan where all followers, except the sick and elderly, needed to fast during the day. Those who can, also make their at least once a lifetime expectation pilgrimage to Mecca in Saudi Arabia for the Hajj. We stayed in both Saudi Arabia and Bahrain. This call to prayer occurs five times each day of the year in Muslim countries. It also occurs in other countries but on a quieter, more private way.

Personally and spiritually, this had a massive impact on me. I had thought before this that my prayer life was going well. Then I experienced this, and it 'blew me away'. I realised how much more I should be doing. How much more I should be including GOD directly in my life. To see GOD as so necessary, that multiple daily prayers are so strongly desired, enhances our personal spirituality and closeness with the One GOD of this world. It was a definite eye-opener for one so integrally a part of the western societal place of religion.

To be fully surrounded by everything Islamic was somewhat of a major challenge for me, but a most beautiful opportunity. So much positivity and growth have come out of this experience for me and my spirituality and religious practice and beliefs.

I realised how much more I should be doing.

How much more I should be including God directly in my life.

To see God as so important, that multiple daily prayers are so strongly desired,

enhances our personal spirituality and closeness with the One God of this world…

I gained so much understanding of prayer through the practice of Islam and two Islamic countries –

Saudi Arabia and Bahrain.

My local Imam back in Australia is a massive strength for Islam.

Religions' Prayer -

Islam, Christianity and Buddhism

Several overseas countries have significantly impacted my prayer life and relationship with GOD and GOD's people worldwide. Three religions, in particular, have impacted strongly on me through various travels overseas. These three religions are Christianity, Islam and Buddhism. Two of these religions pray to one GOD only, i.e. Christianity and Islam, while the third doesn't believe in GOD. Buddhism is a philosophy. Buddhism impressed my wife and me considerably during and after visiting the Buddhist Temple near Tokyo Tower, in Japan. Along with visits to local temples back home. I taught about Buddhism to our senior high school students who studied, Study of Religion in years 11 and 12.

Islam, Saudi Arabia – an extraordinary country and one which inspired me so much, particularly on the prayer front! Along with Bahrain, the country my Dad and I landed in after flying from London; we heard many calls to prayer! This challenges many people's belief in their devotion – it did so for me.

It is the most incredible experience for anyone open to a variety of beliefs and practices. I had previously thought that my Christian prayer life was quite good until landing in these two Arabic, middle-eastern Islamic countries, thirty-three years ago.

My late father was a mining engineer who had to return to Saudi Arabia at El Jabail to oversee any adjustments his rock-solid, salt, mining dredge required. I was his assistant. All worked out very well for all involved.

Christianity, Rome – In The Vatican in Rome – I had an exceptional encounter with the GOD I grew up with as a Christian child. This visit occurred thirteen years ago when my wife and I both turned fifty. I found this experience to be on a similar plane as Islam but in a different religious system. I saw that neither religion, Islam or Christianity, was seen as superior to the other. I was very comfortable accepting this comparison. I had been teaching about Islam for the past few years and Christianity for many years before this as well. I could eventually look back and say that I have taught about the world's five major religions: Christianity, Islam, Judaism, Hinduism and Buddhism for over 30 years.

Buddhism, Tokyo – near Tokyo Tower. The Tokyo Tower in Japan has a spectacular Buddhist temple nearby and close to underneath the Tower. Even though Buddhists don't believe in GOD, I certainly experienced something very unique and special though visiting this Temple. A genuine presence of GOD was felt during this visit, even though there is no GOD in their beliefs and practices. This was a very similar experience when I visited the Rochedale Temple in Brisbane, Australia, and elsewhere worldwide. GOD is strongly felt in many Buddhist Temples?!

Bryan Foster

GOD,
Us
and
LOVE

Why do we want to LIVE a FULL LIFE so Strongly?!

Sounds like a 'dumb' question, do you think???

Why do humans want to live so long and not die? Especially when we get some appreciation of what being with GOD in Heaven is like? Being ONE with the ABSOLUTE LOVE and being encased fully in LOVE with GOD - Forever!

The older we get, the more appreciative of our lives we seem to get. The older we get, the more we appreciate every single day! We know we live on a knife's edge, and anything can happen to us at any time. The world is full of accidents, illnesses and natural and human-made catastrophes and so much more, all of which could end our lives in a second!

By 50 to 60 years of age, most people will have had a few very close encounters where life could be death in a split second. A couple of experiences come to mind quite quickly. The time I was surfing as a seventeen-year-old during a cyclonic surf and was thrown off the ski while at the top of a massive wave and ended up in turbulent waters where I could not see where I was and didn't know up from down. I survived and wondered how and why. Another time was when a bus in Paris almost 'collected' me while about to cross at a pedestrian crossing. I literally almost became a death statistic from being 'hit by a bus'!!!

The more I reflect and interact with nature and goodness and love within our world, the more I love it, and the more robust this love becomes, especially over time.

Yet, I know that Heaven will be so much more. Being unable to fathom this at any depth though, due to my humanity and all its limitations, in a way, helps me desire our world in a very positive, yet limiting way, I realise.

GOD obviously wants us to enjoy the world He deliberately created for us, otherwise why create this and share it with us all? Why guide us, mainly through scripture and prayer, etc., on how to be stewards of creation for all time.

GOD wants us to develop our LOVE of people and nature and try and make each person's life on earth something unique and exceptional. We can't understand why, except it is out of GOD's ABSOLUTE LOVE that it all comes, all created, all shared with us fully! With our LOVE of God and people in return.

Some see it as a trial to see if we are worthy of salvation in Heaven. Others see it as task-driven to develop all those necessary skills needed to make the world a fair and just place for all creation. Etc.

While others will take the cynical route and believe there is no salvation and no GOD. Therefore, greed and lust and all things negative for a 'wholesome', fulfilled life, become the main aim of their lives. They believe that because in their eyes this is the only life and nobody else cares for you, that you should take as much as you can from it and enjoy it yourself or with your loved ones. Wrong!

GOD needs us to chose love over hate, life over death, joy over sorrow, etc. - until that moment in time when GOD calls us home to Heaven. This is where we started and the primary option for where we end after death. Evil ones who deliberately choose evil beliefs and lifestyle and fail to seek forgiveness of GOD for their evil, sinful ways, end up in an eternity of evil – Hell.

Hence, the reason we want to live a fulfilled life comes from GOD out of GOD's ABSOLUTE LOVE and desire for our best.

However, we can not adequately appreciate this, as it comes from divinity, GOD, and we only have our humanity to embrace and understand it as best we can.

Generally, we have an intrinsic feel for this love and these beliefs - and desire it strongly before moving on to GOD at death!

…the reason we want to live a fulfilled life comes from God out of God's ABSOLUTE LOVE and desire for our best.

However, we can not properly appreciate this, as it comes from divinity, God, and we only have our humanity to embrace and understand it as best we can.

Generally, we have an intrinsic feel for this love and these beliefs —

and desire it strongly before moving on to God at death!

Be educated for what is right and truthful

As a good, decent human, we need to be seeking all that is right and truthful. We need to search for good educational sources and people who can best impart to us the correct truth - the truth we need to enhance and better both ourselves and all who we can influence.

What is right? What is truthful?

It is easily considered that what is right is obviously what is not wrong. It is good over the bad. It is the light over the dark. It is GOD's teachings over all the alternatives.

What is truthful is all that comes from GOD. GOD is the light and the truth. It is through GOD that we come to know the truth. It is with GOD's help that we live the truth.

But who will educate us truthfully? Those close to GOD are who we need. Those whose beliefs and lifestyles show that they genuinely believe in GOD and GOD's teachings and are prepared to follow these without reservation in their daily lives. These are not saints, even though that would be ideal. These are everyday people with all their hopes, ambitions and flaws. Who for whatever weaknesses they have still aim to be the best person they can be in the eyes of GOD.

These people could be our parents, our children, our siblings, our neighbour, our friends, our doctor, our dentist, our priest, rabbi, imam, swami, etc. Hopefully, they may be our teachers for that period of our lives, particularly our religion teachers. But as being educated about what is right and truthful is a life-long journey, so many others will impact our search.

It is our obligation to desire this search. To explore what is the best way for us to be educated. To be prepared to change directions when our plans don't work and to continue with whatever does work, while it works.

Finding what is right and truthful is a most freeing and liberating discovery. Becoming that much closer to GOD is a most beautiful experience. It will have significant ramifications on who each of us is as an individual and our place within our family, community and society.

Being educated on what is right and truthful is worth all the effort, setbacks and challenges along the way. It won't be easy, just as nothing worthwhile is easy.

Through prayer, seek GOD's support and help along the way. GOD will lead you and help you know when you discover what is right and truthful.

'Be Truthful'

(First Revelation to Author in 2016)

Bryan Foster

GOD Speaks to Us All – Are We Listening?

GOD speaks to us all. Sometimes it is easy to appreciate the messages for us. Sometimes it takes so much for us to believe that this is even a possibility and then move towards accepting it before genuinely listening and hearing GOD's message for each of us individually and communally.

We are all messengers of GOD with messages for today's world, but we often don't know or believe this. GOD works through people and nature in mysterious ways.

I truly believe what I write about is the TRUTH! It is wonderful to hear GOD's messages for a world in need. Each of us needs to take up GOD's challenging directions.

These are here to make us better, more fulfilled, happy, contented, peace-loving people in the long run. A people who work for these qualities so that these become the norm in all people. Ultimately, the end-game is our salvation with GOD in Heaven.

Is this what we want after we die, for ourselves? For our loved ones? Our families? For our friends and acquaintances? For those, we don't even know, yet?

We can't leave it until the end. That may be too late for us to make the necessary improvements. We need to act now! We need to explore and find GOD and then work on GOD's messages for each of us individually and as part of our communities.

The basic message is: GOD loves us all! GOD loves us so much that we are all called to salvation with GOD in Heaven. We need to accept this invitation in whatever existence and relationship with GOD we find ourselves.

We can't reject GOD!!! Too many believe all go to Heaven. GOD wants all to go to Heaven, yet whoever rejects GOD through their evil beliefs or lifestyles, etc. rejects salvation – outright! Except through a genuine life-changing request for forgiveness from GOD for their evil rejection – right up to that GOD judgement at death.

> God loves us so much that we are all called to salvation with God in Heaven.
>
> We can't reject God!!!
>
> Too many believe all go to Heaven.
>
> God wants all to go to Heaven, yet whoever rejects God through their evil beliefs or lifestyles, etc. rejects salvation – outright!
>
> Except through a genuine life-changing request for forgiveness from God for their evil rejection – right up to that God judgement at death.

(The following seven extracts are Edited Extracts from, *Where's GOD? Revelations Today*, 2018, by Bryan Foster, p167-180.)

GOD

LOVES

YOU - OUTRIGHT

GOD is ABSOLUTE LOVE! GOD LOVES US ABSOLUTELY!

GOD loves you! GOD loves you beyond anything you could imagine!!!

No matter:

who you are

what is your religion

what is your culture

what is your status in life

what is your wealth

where you live

who you live with

what you do for work

what you do in life

how you decide

how you do things

why you do things

who you mix with

why you mix with them

what is your past

what is your present

what is your future

what you have done wrong

whatever, whoever, wherever, why ever,

whenever... GOD loves you!

How good is that to hear!? Couldn't we listen to that over and over!? Why? Because it's true!!! It's inspiring! It's divine!

GOD loves us no matter what we do. GOD won't always agree with our choices. But these are our choices, and we have to live with these. Each of us is responsible for our actions.

There are times when we are forced to make decisions, not of our own making. It is unfortunate but a real aspect of life. People affect us and influence us, often in forceful or subtle ways. Maybe nature made life's choices difficult for us sometimes. These instances make us react and respond in various ways. How we do, this is our decision and affects our relationship with GOD and others.

We must never forget that GOD still loves us no matter what we do. We are the ones who choose to move away from GOD through our thoughts or actions. Even then, GOD doesn't leave us alone. We can always return to GOD for love and support. Forgiveness is an essential aspect of our lives with each other, ourselves and with GOD.

This is nothing new. It has always been and always will be. Why are so many people today so confused or even refuse to believe that there is even a GOD? GOD loves you!

I

CAN'T

STOP

REPEATING -

GOD'S

ABSOLUTE

LOVE

FOR

ALL

OF

US

EXISTS

FOREVER - EQUALLY

WE LET OURSELVES DOWN WHEN
WE SIN, WHICH TURNS US AWAY
FROM GOD.

**GOD DOESN'T TURN AWAY
FROM US! EVER!!!**

But - Life's Not Fair.

Life is not fair, even with all the love that exists within each person and the world as a whole. Life indeed isn't fair in the sense we commonly use it. But...

It's very easy to sit back in a first world country and complain about how tough life is. Maybe we could spend some time in a third world country living their lifestyle on their means and then ask how fair life is. Many in third world countries could do likewise in their own countries and then see others who are worse off than themselves.

Life's fairness is so relative.

We all expect the best for ourselves and our loved ones. We would probably go to exceptional lengths to make this occur. And in many cases already do.

How then can we legitimately complain about fairness when billions are far worse off?

What is fairness anyway? Is it equality of wealth and opportunities? Is it empathy for all fellow humans? Is it social justice for all? Is it all these and more?

Even in countries which have virtually everything needed, such as in many western countries, life is not fair. Even when the great majority of these people stand up for their justice system, health and education systems, social services and welfare systems, police and security systems, wage system, and freedoms beyond so many other countries, there is still an avalanche of social injustice. Add to this the egalitarianism, equality and opportunities for all found in a few countries, and there are still various problems of fairness remaining.

Someone born into a wealthy, educated, powerful family is far more likely to have a comfortable life; to have so many life and career opportunities. To have the chance to marry into other wealthy, influential families. To have so much that their understanding of the poor is mostly compromised to support their elitism's regime.

The view that some have this or that because of hard work and that those others who don't have the essentials can only blame themselves for their problems is SO wrong. It is hard to argue that people want similar things, yet life's choices or inevitabilities end up differently for each person. Those fortunate enough to gain more often don't want to share much of it, while those who ended up with less would like the others to share. This is an argument so based on where a person stands on the wealth continuum. Unfair for the poor! Not fair for the wealthy - who have so much more and don't need anything like what they have.

Unfortunately, most rich people think the poor are in control of their lives. They use this to justify doing no more for them than necessary. It allows these people with so much to sleep comfortably, guiltfree. Who would choose poverty and deprivation over wealth and power? Who would not choose motivated, successful parents, family and friends to guide and shape their every move and development and literally be role models of the wealthy? Who would not choose a good education at a good school followed by an excellent tertiary qualification? And the choices go on…

Fairness is about so many aspects of life, not just money. We need to consider all elements associated with a population's health, education, career opportunities and enhancements, societal relationships, equality before the law, access to adequate housing, clothing, temperature control, pollution control and other environmental effects on people. In fact, in all aspects of life that impact and affect each person. It is also a significant amount more than just looking after culture, nation, community or religious group, etc. It is totally about looking after each within their community.

Is GOD unfair to people? NO!!!

People choose to be unfair to each other, out of their God-given Free Will.

Overall, life is fair in the sense that our lives are GOD-given for us to do as we find possible and loving. To do to others and the whole of creation, as we find possible and loving. The fairness begins with each of us from reaching the age of reason, around 7-9 years of age. Life is fair in GOD's eyes as we are created equal and placed in this world together. Of course, there is an aspect of mystery, e.g. why were we placed where and when we were and in our particular circumstances? People (not God) take the fairness out of life – mostly due to greed, the second Revelation given by God to me (and possibly others worldwide) in May 2016 – 'Don't Be Greedy'.

We all know what needs to be done, but how many do the hard things? The strict sharing, caring, equalising things needed for fairness worldwide? The real, life-saving, empathetic, loving necessities all people need to do and accept.

If people were sincere (the First Revelation from God in May 2016 – Be truthful), they would accept that they are greedy, placing themselves first and others down the line as a generalisation. Most wouldn't see it this way and would probably argue against it. Why? For the unfair people, it's easier to deny than accept. To accept will likely mean a significant life-change for the rich, who by far don't care too much about the poor in general.

Here's the big question. When was the last time you split your assets with others so that each person could live a fair and just existence?

GOD must allow all our choices to occur because we have been given absolute freedom out of GOD's absolute love for us to choose GOD's way through our informed conscience or the other way. Because GOD loves us absolutely, we have to have total freedom to choose from GOD or evil. We have been given the rules and guidelines on how to live successful, rewarding lives for all. Fairness dictates that we must choose God! If not, evil would be untruthful and greedy.

No, life's not fair anywhere!

Greed rules. Privilege rules. Power and Money talk!

The most disappointing reality to all of this is that there are enough resources worldwide for all people to live real, comfortable lives EVERYWHERE. But all people have to share their excesses. Excesses being resources beyond the necessities. All people need to be TRULY generous and loving and empathetic. Most people could share their excesses, yet how many could share a more realistic, more generous amount to give the poor a good, loving life?

Unfortunately, we all know this will probably never happen, as stated above. People's nature, nationalism, greed, and generally speaking a real dislike by the haves with helping the huge majority of others, the have-nots. But many of humanity are forever hopeful that this will occur in our lifetimes.

Can it start? Yes. Can it happen to a degree? Yes. It's up to us to do our own thing to help, financially, politically, socially, etc. Give it a go! You won't know how good it is until you are a part of what should be a massive movement – eventually!

GOD loves all people equally and needs us to do likewise. To give everyone a fair go. So that life can be fair!

It is from this place onwards that fairness begins to disappear, mainly due to humanity's choices. Sometimes it could be due to the fate of natural events beyond our control. Part of the mystery of GOD and what GOD places before each of us. (See also 'Suffering - Don't Blame GOD')

The most disappointing reality to all of this is that
there are enough resources worldwide
for all people to live real,
comfortable lives EVERYWHERE.

But all people, except the very poor, have to share
Not just their excesses
but a considerable amount from their everyday accounts/lifestyle.
Fairness isn't cheap!
But fairness is essential for true LOVE!

You Can't Have Everything No Entitlements

It seems such an obvious statement, yet so many these days believe they can have, be, do everything they so desire! They lose any sense of realism by being caught up with so much marketing and well-being, goal setting, dreaming hype. Aiming to be our realistic best is crucial.

It is so much a less stressful, rewarding, self-fulfilled lifestyle when one accepts that there will be limitations, unbeatable challenges, fewer opportunities than expected. To not always want and need more than is realistically possible or even desirable is liberating. Being real is real!

The notion that if I dream it and want it badly enough, and work towards it, then it WILL become real is often so off the mark. Just ask some challenging questions, e.g. could I ever become an astronaut at my age — answer no. No matter what I dream, work towards, want, 'need', this can never happen. Why? Primarily because of my age and health! Probably also because I would not be able to gain the proper training required, etc. You might argue, well, it is different for young people. Yes, for some but not for most. Suppose you don't have the academic, intellectual, physical and emotional characteristics needed for such an endeavour. In that case, it doesn't matter how much dreaming, working hard, and dedication you aim for, it just can't happen. It is also the case for many other career moves. How many young people believe they are being belittled not yet being their company's 'go-to' person? How many don't think you have to start at an appropriate level, which isn't a manager or even the CEO?

The young, and many not so young, are facing such strong family and significant adult support and developing a sense of entitlement well beyond reality. Too many helicopter parents do so much for their children that their children miss the opportunities to work hard, make mistakes, take responsibility for their actions, and become better people. Too many adults want their children to be so 'successful' that they don't give them the foundations needed to achieve success in its most real sense.

People need to have dreams, goals and hope for future 'prosperity and success', realistically - Aim high. Work hard. Be the best you can be. But be real. Realise that there are limitations and lack of opportunities. But always be on the lookout and be ready for the right options when these come. But always be aware of what makes you truly happy and content. Excesses don't do this, e.g. materialism and excessive power, don't do this.

Good people who genuinely care about you and your well-being will be your authentic support. Be on the lookout for those who want excesses for themselves and you. Do they know what is best for themselves? For you? Or are they also trapped in the unreality of excess and other associated unrealistic expectations?

GOD is our best guide and support. Keep in contact with GOD, primarily through prayer, and be aware of what GOD wants for you. GOD has a plan for each of us. Keep doing what you inherently feel is right, comforting, personally rewarding, and best for you as an individual, and as an essential family and community member. God's place will become known to you over time.

We need to ask GOD to help us, support us and bring us peace and prosperity in its most real sense. Remember that GOD wants the best for you and is always there for you. Just ask. We were created to be the best we can become. No two of us are the same. When we open ourselves to what GOD wants for us and go along with it, there develops a real, authentic, comforting sense of peace and fulfilment. You become one with GOD in this world.

All People are Equal in GOD's Eyes

All are created equal and should have similar quality lifestyles, no matter the prevailing political system, culture or religion in operation.

GOD has no favourites. Everyone is equal. Every single creation is perfect in GOD's eyes. Each person needs to have all the same rights and privileges as each other. There are no exceptions for any reason! To believe otherwise breaks GOD's teachings and commandments.

These divine messages are simple. GOD is absolutely awesome beyond belief and needs to be seen, respected and treated as such by all people. All people need to be treated equally by each other, just as GOD treats them equally.

When it comes to those who aren't treated this way, GOD acts and tells us to do likewise. GOD is especially with and in the poor, destitute and all the disadvantaged. Apart from loving each of us equally, another reason is that their lives can be equalised to be like others. There needs to be a massive positive change in this world for people to be equal - in all countries, cultures, religions and groups.

Why is it that most adolescents (teens to mid-20s) favour social justice for all? Why do they seek a noble cause and then fight for this with a passion? Why is this trait so inherent in people? It is often attained even when parents actively do everything in their power to stop it. It becomes a matter for the haves to fight so hard for their advantages. Otherwise, they may end up without some or most of it. How could any wealthy person live a happy, successful life, with just the basics? Easily - especially when many or most are doing the same and being as FAIR as possible!

We all have Divine Eyes

Nothing is more beautiful than our divine eyes! Nothing allows a vision of the true humanity of someone more than through these lenses. The eyes say it all! The eyes are indeed the window to a person's soul. To the real self. To our oneness with GOD.

Through the eyes is where you get to see where someone is. It is very difficult if not impossible for someone to fake their eyes and the messages they are sending through these. The overall appearance, the use of the eyelids, surrounding frowns, smiles, etc., can change and be acted differently, hence giving a different message. The overall facial appearance may be real or fake. The visible eyes, including the iris and pupil, are the conduit to the true self.

We sense where and when the person is genuine and authentic, truthful and loving through the eyes. There is a GOD-given depth seen through the eyes. The more genuine, loving and egalitarian a person, the more this is viewed 'within' through the eyes.

The eyes' irises are considered the most beautiful aspect of each person's physical self. These encompass their physical colourings and intimate aspects of personal characteristics, including speckles, colour variations and other intricate designs.

Loving, genuine, authentic people shine through their eyes. Holiness is seen in the eyes. GOD is seen in the eyes. You can get a real sense of the divine through the eyes of loving people who are close to GOD. This concept of the eyes being the window to the soul has its basis in the New Testament, Mt 6:22-23 and in a quote attributed to Cicero, over 100 years prior.

Roman philosopher Cicero (1st century BCE) highlights how the eyes interpret what's happening in the mind. (Oxford Reference)

Matthew is more specific than Cicero. He highlights that both goodness, light, and evil, darkness, will be seen through the eyes. Therefore, the eyes being the 'lamp' to the soul.

"The eye is the lamp of the body. So, if your eye is healthy, your whole body will be full of light; but if your eye is unhealthy, your whole body will be full of darkness. If then the light in you is darkness, how great is the darkness!" (Mt 6:22-23, NRSV)

Conversely, as seen through both the evangelists who wrote Matthew and the philosopher Cicero, our true selves when evil/dark and lacking in love, will also be seen through our eyes, when we have chosen to move away from GOD through our beliefs and actions, we move into the darkness, to the evil.

Our eyes tell this story, especially for those aware and who have a well-developed intuitive sense. You may even get a sense from someone who can't look a good person in the eye. There seems to be this natural turning away from the light /goodness/GODness!

It is as if the 'sun' is too bright for the evil/dark ones. That darkness is where the comfort lies for these people. To come out into the light becomes a real struggle for them.

This is exactly what GOD wants from and for them - to come into the light. To see the error of their ways. To seek forgiveness and to become one with all other loving, authentic, loving people, GOD-people.

Our eyes are genuinely the windows to our soul. To our real selves.

GOD'S LOVE

The Solution is GOD's Love

Love will heal to a degree depending on God's view and our personal, worldly problems. But this needs to be true love seen for what it is and the source of this love is GOD. GOD needs to be turned to for guidance, support and strength. Only a GOD-assisted revolution-of-love will be successful! Humans do not have the capacity or will to do this on their own! Just consider the amount of violence and war in our world today.

The longer-lasting successes throughout history have had GOD as their supporter. Evil has had limited control at various times, but these were defeated by a loving God-inspired and supported reaction. Or a loving action in preparation for, or anticipation of, an evil event.

A misunderstanding of GOD's place in the world leads not only to ignorance of GOD but of what our role is, as well.

GOD is Absolute Love. GOD gives us Absolute Free Will. We decide so much for ourselves. Our personal and communal actions affect so many and so much of what happens in this world. Yes, this cannot explain everything GOD does or allows to happen. There is definitely an aspect of faith and mystery.

As humans, we cannot expect to appreciate and understand GOD much at all. GOD is divine; we are human – a significant distinction and differentiation. It is not until we reach perfection with GOD in Heaven will we genuinely know GOD. However, we can learn so much about GOD from religious history, history, religious teachings, nature, prayer, etc.

With all this complexity, GOD is with us and wants the best for all of us. We must work with GOD towards the equality of all. Those who disagree with equality disagree with GOD.

Forgiveness from GOD and Others is Love

Forgiveness is the most challenging process but an essential need of all humans to live with love. The stronger the use of forgiveness, the greater will be the love of self and others.

People need to forgive others for their wrongdoing towards them. Others need to forgive us for our failings. We need to forgive ourselves. Forgiveness offered and received is essential for the relationship to repair.

Of course, this is not a simple procedure or one with an inevitable outcome. It depends on so much. It depends on our openness to forgive and to be forgiven. It depends on the person we hurt, or who hurt us, being open to forgive, or accepting forgiveness. It sometimes depends on our ability to offer restitution knowingly or unknowingly to the recipient. It depends on our experience of forgiveness and how we have been affected previously. It depends on our personality, mental, physical and social health, on our standing with the person concerned, and on so much more. Those who know love can forgive. Forgiveness is essential for love to be real, positive and empathetic, etc.

Once we can forgive and be forgiven and affect restitution, if necessary, we are set free. We can live more peaceful, fulfilling lives. Our relationships are more robust, and we are happier within these. We are more complete as people living in our families, workplaces, communities, etc.

We must also appreciate and accept GOD into our earthly relationships. We need to invite GOD into our relationships, to help strengthen these and be there when difficulties arise. When this happens, GOD supports us and helps us work through the challenges, until the final loving outcome is achieved.

Primarily, out of love, we are required to place GOD as the number one in our lives and our relationships. When we can accept this, and turn our relationships over to GOD, we are then open to receive so much assistance willingly and accept the outcomes, as part of GOD's plan.

This is very freeing and something towards which we need to work.

Apologising to GOD for our hurt caused and the wrongdoings done, adds another dimension to our improvement and relationship with GOD. GOD always wants the best for each of us. GOD knows intrinsically that we will weaken and make mistakes, hurting ourselves and others along the way. We can't hurt GOD, but we can freely move away from GOD (sin) through our thoughts and actions. Our acknowledgement of these wrongs and hurts helps the healing process and brings us back closer to our GOD relationship. It is GOD's loving desire for us.

GOD loves each of us so much that GOD needs us all to be as close as possible to each other and GOD - in true love.

Once we can forgive and be forgiven...

we are set free.

We are able to live more peaceful, fulfilling and loving lives together.

GOD's Revelations for Today's World

The five previous books in this *'GOD Today' Series* primarily explored the twenty-one Revelations from GOD to the author. Each one was detailed in *Where's GOD? Revelations Today*. While the first essential one was highlighted in the first book, *1GOD.world: One GOD for All,* i.e. there is only 1 GOD forever for all people, cultures and religions. Book 5, *Jesus and Mahomad are God*, highlighted the next most extraordinary Revelation #15, as shown in the book's title. The latest photobook, Book 4, *Where's GOD? Revelations Today Photobook Companion: GOD Signs* explores the signs and coincidences given by GOD to the author. These provide various justifications for being genuine Revelations needed for a divided world – TODAY.

The first fifteen Revelations were received on 29 May, 2016 on the plains of Mt Warning, Australia. (See Appendix 2 - Mt Warning – Word of GOD Revealed to the Author – the Story)

Before this on my 25th birthday, I lovingly received GOD when Sr Ann prayed over by teaching at a co-educational secondary school in Brisbane on their Commitment to God Day. (See Appendix 1, Where it all Began – Author's 25th birthday)

The critical reasons for believing that these Revelations and inspired messages are from GOD will be explained in more detail (See *Appendix 4* - Are the Revelations and inspired messages contained in this series, the *'GOD Today' Series*, the Truth from God?)

The specific reasons are:

- the 25th birthday experience of GOD in May 1982

- the longevity without any personal doubt of this strong association with GOD;
- the Tears from GOD experiences, which have been growing in intensity and frequency, especially in the most recent years (See *Where's GOD? Revelations Today* p. 46-50);
- the Revelations from GOD at the foot of Mt Warning in May 2016;
- the recent photographic images highlighting metaphorical or direct links with GOD
- coincidences and signs from GOD over many years (See explanations at *Where's GOD? Revelations Today* p. 148-162; See images throughout *Where's GOD? Revelations Today Photobook Companion: GOD Signs*)
- the personal career/vocation, 40 years teaching religion from years 1-12, including 30 years of Study of Religion to senior years;
- holding senior leadership positions in religious schools and parishes;
- prayer and meditation throughout and
- the continued strong support and agreement from my wife, Karen.

Each of these reasons supports the belief in the Revelation or inspired messages being from GOD. GOD never forces anyone to believe anything. There is a level of 'proof' and the mystery of the faith with any Revelation or inspired message from GOD. Therefore, through the combinations of these reasons and others, GOD's unique presence is experienced with the outcomes of each needed to be shared. Having always been close to GOD, or at least in my teens on the fringes, allows for that openness to hear and know intrinsically when something is legitimately from GOD.

21 Revelations from God to the Author 2016(15) & 2018(6)

In the order revealed.

Revelation #15 was edited to summarise its fundamental concepts to gain its title and released in August, 2020 as *Jesus and Mahomad are God.*

GOD has directed this to be so. GOD certainly acts in mysterious ways, which can not be challenged or questioned. Out of faith, this timeline will be met as directed also.

The first 15 Revelations are detailed in Book 3 - *Where's GOD? Revelations Today* p.61-112.

** These points with stars were joined together for Revelation #15 on the original Revelation from God in 2016.

Revelations #16 to #21 - Another six Revelations were received at Mt Warning Rainforest Park on November 3, 2018.

('Mahomad' and 'Mahommad' were spelt these ways when the Revelations were received from God in 2016. Punctuation is as presented by God.)

1. Be truthful

2. Don't be Greedy

3. Love life – don't take it

4. Respect all

5. Love one another as I have loved you

6. Die for what is right

7. Be educated for what is right & truthful

8. Education is paramount for all

9. We are one

10. One GOD only One GOD

11. GOD's messages to a world in need

12. This world is in enormous need

13. Cyberbullying – in all its forms, of all sorts, of all ages…

14. Fear rules – often from the cyber world eliminate this

15. ** Jesus is GOD

Brahma is God

Yahweh is God

** Mahomad is Allah/God

** Don't doubt this

Jesus and Mahomad is God

Mahommad is Allah is God

16.   We need GOD

17.   We need <u>to be vulnerable to GOD</u>

18.   We need to continually be asking

for GOD's help and assistance

& support – always.

'No big heads' – Just ask for
help. Always.

19.   We are insignificant compared to
GOD.

20.   GOD is so so superior – face up to it

Believe it! Stop fighting it!

21.   Be meek & humble & real

(Spelling and grammar as presented to the author by GOD.)

'Live for Greatness' - Live for GOD

I have just been considering the reality of GOD in our world, especially the digital world that so many of us now actually populate to a ridiculously high level. So you can imagine that it came as quite a shock to read the advert on the back of a newspaper's feature magazine lying next to me.

This magazine featured a world-renowned watch with the caption, "Live for Greatness".

Oh, what a clash! The secular world is screaming for us to buy an expensive watch so that we can - "live for greatness"!

What could be the greatness to which we are invited through having this watch on our wrists? Maybe we could look COOL!!! Whatever this may mean?! We could perhaps look wealthy?! No doubt wealth is the answer to the meaning of life - not! So could there possibly be any other reason?

Humorously, maybe we could wear the watch and time we spent with the most critical existence in this world? But time is irrelevant to this reality! OK - let's lose the watch! It is not important!!!

Let's encompass GOD fully! Let's live for greatness - for GOD!!! Let's let GOD give us the time of our lives! Let's LOVE GOD honestly and allow GOD to LOVE US fully.

Nothing can beat the time we spend with GOD - nothing! GOD is especially present in our time with our spouse. He is especially present in our time with our family and friends. GOD is present when we live in the present. He is present in our time with nature, in fun times, in everyday times.

However, GOD is most especially present in our time with 'Him'!!! Prayer!!! Silence!!! GOD!!!

To have this most personal and inner reality challenged by a very secular advertisement causes me to pause and reflect thoughtfully on all that is important in life. It challenges me to re-evaluate all that is most important to me!

Through this challenge came a new inner realisation that I must be strong, very strong, in not only accepting what is right but to accept this truth in all that it is - GOD's presence and invitation in this wonderful world of ours. Being distracted away from the truth is oh so easy! Being able to stay with the innermost important message and reality in my life, GOD, is so significant. No distraction can be allowed to get in the way!

GOD is real! GOD watches over us! Go, GOD!

Let's encompass God fully!

Let's live for Greatness - for God!!!

Let's let God give us the time of our lives!

Let's LOVE GOD honestly and allow GOD to LOVE US fully.

Love One Another as I Have Loved You

Never has a greater commandment been uttered so much to assist people in their relationships with one another. GOD had resent it to the author in 2016. I would presume it would also have been sent to many other people throughout history and the world.

Whether it is taken in its true context or taken as one person's relationship with another person, the message is unambiguous - love each other as the ultimate lover, Jesus loved and loves everyone equally.

To love each other as we would like to be loved ourselves will free us to be ourselves truly. To forgive, show compassion and understanding, see the best in others, and allow each person to be him/herself entirely is what true love enables.

(The exception maybe for those who unfortunately have not experienced true love and/or are unable to express genuine love with others.)

The superficial in relationships becomes insignificant. Someone's appearance, career, financial status, possessions, etc., are seen as irrelevant to a truly loving relationship. Superficiality loses its lustre. Reality rules! The real person is seen for what they truly are - a unique creation with so much to offer humanity.

The loving Jesus showed by his word and lifestyle what true love is. So much so that he even died for humanity's sake! He showed me how to love deeply! How to lovingly forgive those who hurt you! How to live love in family relationships. How to assist those who are not as well-off or as fortunate as yourself. He showed that helping physically, mentally, emotionally and spiritually ill is extremely important.

To share everything is a massive challenge for us who are part of a materialistic and consumer-based society. But if we are to love genuinely, we must be prepared to reach out and assist others with time, goods and finances, etc., as well as to be prepared to share and be helped when we need it in return.

This new loving world is not one where we hide behind high walls or in cocooned apartment blocks, where we fear for our lives or personal protection, where we think selfishly and live accordingly - where darkness hides the light.

This is a world where we come out from behind both physical and metaphorical walls into the light. This is where darkness, selfishness and greed are left behind. It is where true love exists and where each is treated with respect and lovingly encouraged to be their authentic self!

To love one another as I have loved you is the call to enter the light - to be our authentic selves supported by the right light.

.

> …the message is extremely clear –
>
> love each other as the ultimate lover,
>
> Jesus, loved and loves.

Old-Age and GOD

As people get closer to going home to GOD, there is a final development stage as they become as close to GOD as possible before death. This is also when these people clear the decks of their negative, sinned record and turn to GOD for significant assistance in growing back if necessary towards GOD before their deaths.

It is often so difficult to ascertain where certain older folk are in their progress towards GOD?

However, we know from GOD that all people are welcomed home to Heaven if they genuinely want to and have forgiven their sins. Every set of authentic scriptures for each genuine religion points to the equal LOVE GOD has for all people, no matter their beliefs or state in which they are currently living. The divine desire is for everyone's salvation. To get everyone to be with GOD in Heaven after they have died.

This whole stage of life is refocussed on closure with the world and moving onto that next stage. The ultimate stage is of GOD and GOD's people once again becoming one with GOD in Heaven. This closeness with GOD is something GOD wants.

This is the whole purpose of the afterlife, to be one with GOD in Heaven forever once again when we die.

The younger we are, the more difficult it is to understand and appreciate this end of life stage. And conversely, for the older we get. We appear to be once again more childlike and look forward to our new eternity, and strive to become close to GOD so that at our death, we will hopefully choose to be with GOD through making our forgiveness with GOD. (See the previous page for detail.)

Jesus was Right – of Course!

A Unique Example from Today's World – poverty vs. wealth!

Jesus was right. Trust in GOD for your survival and salvation. My first response is how pathetic it is to say it like that... imagine ever questioning Jesus' teachings?! A most confrontational beginning to a book, I am sure. "How dare you!" Some would say. "Go on; explain yourself!" Others may say. Maybe, just maybe, others would see it as a challenge and ask for more explanation.

This story was written while my wife, Karen, and I were touring around the driest continent on this planet, Australia, in 2014. We had travelled over 16000km, from lush, spectacular beaches, through various state city capitals, country cities, and towns, wealthy and poor regions, various bushlands, crossed many rivers, some with water, climbed numerous rock formations, walked dry river beds, admired national natural icons such as Uluru (Ayers Rock) in the centre, experienced the indigenous people in their homelands throughout the country, been challenged by illness, and celebrated so many memorable moments together – to name but a few, that we feel so absolutely privileged to have such a lifetime opportunity.

The reality of what turned out to be the yet unknown main purpose of our adventure came while we were sitting in the Katherine, Northern Territory, Hospital's Accident and Emergency room. Katherine is a poor town in the north-central part of the Northern Territory. Its population is mostly transient and tourist-based. Yet, a large number of indigenous first peoples live there permanently. It is the crossroads for those travelling north to Darwin, south to Uluru or South Australia, east to Queensland, and west to Western Australia. Thousands of grey nomads (the name given to mostly retired folk who travel

Australia in their caravans and four-wheeled drive cars for around six months each year) and pass through Katherine on their way to far distant places from their homes. Katherine is also adjacent to Nitmiluk, a series of spectacular gorges with its caravan camping park and high-quality resort. Katherine and surrounds are a contrast of cultures, lifestyles, and various extreme levels of wealth. The difference between my typical inner-city experiences at Australia's most popular beachside tourist destination and my home of the Gold Coast, Queensland, could be no further from the reality I was experiencing in this hospital in Katherine, even if I had tried to plan it that way.

This hospital experience was the first time in my life that my wife and I had, for quite a significant time that day, been surrounded by over twenty first peoples in the hospital waiting room. These twenty beautiful people were also there for various personal needs, from medical to social assistance. I have never felt so at home, so close to others, so one with the moment, than at this time. I also felt the paradox of what it must be like for minorities; to feel quite different from others yet requiring the same attention. We were all treated equally and attended to as we needed to be by the hospital staff. After a few hours, I was greeted by a smiling young African woman doctor and was one with my world and its people. The loving journey over many years of incredible experiences and opportunities to this personal and spiritual place will be considered throughout this book's *Series*.

The confrontational paradox in the waiting room brought a silent gasp as my inner self realised the importance of a particular moment. We had been sitting there for around two hours and had gained quite an appreciation of those around us, from small children, their mothers, fathers, and grandparents, right through to one 75-year-old aboriginal man named Billy. Billy had been a challenge for the nursing staff trying to assist him. His main health issue causing this concern was his degree of deafness and inability to communicate effectively. He was continually agitated and worried over a long period about getting to see a doctor. He would be up and down to the triage nurse wanting to know how his progress in the line was going. Unfortunately, when Billy finally got to see the doctor, he soon walked out of his consultation, claiming his deafness affected the doctor's proper treatment of him. Following this, he would continually approach the triage nurse's window again, pace around the waiting room, and be in and out of the hospital, trying to get to the doctor again. You could feel the genuine concern of all in the hospital, staff and patients alike. Throughout this, the television on the wall was showing inane soap operas, except for exciting tourist destination filler ads. The confrontational paradox occurred during a tourist destination filler highlighting my home city of the spectacular Gold Coast. (By this stage of the journey, I had not been home for over two months, so I was quite missing it.) During one particular filler scene, a brilliant sequence showing the glamorous and spectacularly beautiful Surfers Paradise beach and surf, Billy walked immediately under the television screen.

This contrasting image defined a paradox, which was extremely palpable. The vast richness of opportunity, beauty, wealth, and weather in the Gold Coast was suddenly contrasted with the enormous struggles suffered by the Australian outback's first peoples. My gasp was palpable and audible. I was stunned! I hurt for Billy and his people. I was embarrassed at all I had and could have – from personal relations, professional opportunities, health, education, lifestyle and wealth, etc. I wanted to scream for Billy and his people!

At this moment in the Australian outback, I finally realised that you don't need much, just the necessities. This Gold Coast kid who had become a middle-aged grandfather had his values and priorities turned upside-down. It is acknowledged that each culture and country is unique and quite similar at times in these requirements. I would hazard a guess though, that the Australian city dweller's high-quality lifestyle and opportunities would be possibly close to the top of the international rankings. Therefore, I can relate to those from such highly affluent countries and what they need and what they could do for others less fortunate. The more you travel internationally, the more you realise how tough it is for most people and how unfair life is for them.

It is tough to say, but unfortunately, most of us are basically greedy people in these wealthy countries. Our cultures have brought us to this position. Our political and economic models based on capitalism and materialism cause us to strive for so much, actually believing this to be necessary for a successful and happy existence. Many well-off hope or are close to acknowledging this but are too scared to accept the challenge. It will take an earth-shattering experience for this to become a reality for them. I have had my earth-shattering experiences, which I would like to share throughout this text and this *Series*. I finally believe that it is possible to go beyond these culturally-induced beliefs to a more fulfilling and rewarding existence for all.

This personal journey has been influenced by significant events, mainly health, average Australian wealth, and professional issues, over the past few years. My wife, Karen, and I journeyed through the 17000km of travel through Australia in a 5.5 x 2m space called a caravan/trailer. We peaked during the paradoxical experience in the Katherine Hospital. It was a growth process, which continues to develop as we continue journeying around Australia and experiencing so many diverse people, places, and cultures. This is a personal journey, yet one mostly shared with Karen. It got to such a stage where it felt better shared than just kept to ourselves.

That others may have similar journeys and outcomes, which also need to be shared, or at least supported, to accept such beliefs as real and attainable.

We have now lived in a 5.5m x 2m space for five months - successfully! A caravan/trailer. I accept that there often are other conditions which add to the whole experience, e.g., a toilet and shower block in some caravan parks we visit. All we need extra, though, is a toilet for '#2s'. We often don't have a shower block but will always have at least a drop-pit toilet for the mornings. We very much enjoy bush camping away from caravan parks as well.

Expenses are much lower while on the road travelling. Our highest costs at this stage are the ones we get associated with our house in the city from which we come, e.g., mortgage, rates, utilities, pool cleaning, mowing, and fuel, etc. We lease it out while travelling.

So from where did this great revelation about trust and needs come? The journey to where we now begin decades ago while studying to become a Catholic school teacher while at a Catholic teacher's college. Various scriptural and theological subjects and subsequent discussions, essays, and examinations, challenged our very notion of existence in this capitalistic, first world of resources and opportunities of ours – the western world. So far away from the other earthly worlds, a world had little possibility of significantly impacting them and improving their lifestyles. Were we to become puppets of our society, pandering to the slick advertisements and marketing strategies, or were we to be challenged by the teachings of Jesus and other holy people/prophets from most religions, so clearly stated in their scriptures and theologies? Were we going to teach what we had been taught to perpetuate the cultural mores of the time? Were we to continue the next generation on to such a path?

Bryan Foster

These times challenged each of us to think outside the box, somewhat differently from most people in society. Sad to say, though, as young people ourselves then, to appreciate the ramifications of such challenges were minimal, by and large. We continued with the way society was heading. Sure we supported various street demonstrations for equality; for protection from nuclear-powered plants and possible environmental disasters; for the right to march and have our say (in the days of a state premier who believed otherwise and that he was the font of all wisdom and to trust in him implicitly), to end the war in Vietnam, etc. These truly were heady days - days to let our local world know what we thought about its direction. No internet and massive social media campaigns here – not yet invented. Calculators were as good as we got back then. Everything this generation needed, e.g., the mass media of newspapers, television, and radio, required to be on-board for any social/environmental messages to reach the large population. Yet none of this truly impacted the great majority worldwide, suffering from inequality, poverty, starvation, disease, malnutrition, minimal human rights/social justice, etc.

The next challenge was to place all this in the context of the teachings of GOD. To go and explore scripture and to find examples that support such inherent feelings and beliefs. The first quote is a beautiful story and one which has been used as an inspirationally spiritual message:

"Therefore I tell you, do not worry about your life, what you will eat or what you will drink, nor about your body, what you will wear. Is not life more than food and the body more than clothing? Look at the birds of the air; they neither sow nor reap nor gather into barns, and yet your heavenly Father feeds them. Are you not of more value than they? And can any of you, by worrying, add a single hour to your span of life? And why do you worry about clothing? Consider the lilies of the field, how they grow; they neither toil nor spin, yet I tell you, even Solomon in all his glory was not clothed like one of these. But if GOD so clothes the grass of the field, which is alive today and tomorrow is thrown into the oven, will he not much more clothe you-you of little faith? Therefore do not worry, saying, 'What will we eat?' or 'What will we drink?' or 'What will we wear?' For it is the Gentiles who strive for all these things, and indeed your heavenly Father knows that you need all these things.

But seek first for the kingdom of GOD and his righteousness, and all these things will be given to you as well… So do not worry about tomorrow, for tomorrow will bring worries of its own. Today's trouble is enough for today." (Matthew 6: 25-34 NRSV)

It was at this moment, in the Australian outback, at the public hospital in Katherine in the NT,

that I finally realised that you don't need much, just the necessities.

This Gold Coast 'kid', who had become a middle-aged grandfather, had his values and priorities turned upside-down.

To the correct position!

My gasp was palpable and audible.

I was stunned!

I hurt for Billy (an elderly Australian First People) and his people.

I was embarrassed at all I had and could have – from personal relations, professional opportunities, education, lifestyle, health and wealth, etc.

I wanted to scream for Billy and his people!

Where

is

GOD'S

LOVE?

Moonbeam Capture

A metaphor for our uniqueness, unity, and closeness with GOD.

Wherever you are, you cannot escape the capture of the moonbeam. See how this book's moonshine cover centres you.

As you look towards the moon on a clear night, you become the centre of its gleaming light. You are the one literally in the centre! No-one in this world is at the centre of the light shining on you! You are extremely special!

An excellent metaphor of GOD signalling you out! You are a special one! You are the full focus of GOD's attention - you are it!

Everyone is unique in the eyes of GOD. The moonlight metaphorically shows this more than anything else. Wherever you move, no matter the speed, no matter the time, you are always at the centre! You cannot escape this centeredness. No matter how hard you try, you are still at the centre of the moonbeam - the centre of GOD's metaphorical and real attention!

This is an exceptional invitation to realise the reality of GOD and the place you play in this loving relationship.

Another reality could be experienced when under the influence of a direct ray of sunlight. With all its power and heat and intensity, this awesome sunbeam says much to us about GOD and GOD's relationship with each person.

GOD loves us so much that 'He' wants us to respond to the loving-kindness, compassion, and forgiveness being divinely offered to each of us.

If we can find GOD metaphorically in the warmth and the power of the sun, or the gentle peacefulness and quiet of the moonbeam, we are open to experience the real GOD in our lives!

GOD is calling us to be in a unique oneness with 'Him'! Calling us to be unique, yet an integral part of all humankind and calling us to be totally human within His loving embrace!

The moonbeam and sunbeam are just two of GOD's many worldly signs used as invitations to us. GOD is not only found in nature but those extra special natural events and happenings. Those 'Wow' moments! Those moments when we just have to challenge ourselves to respond to such invitations with a loud, "Yes!"

The moonbeam and the silence of the light gleaming over the sea towards us, as we sit quietly on the seashore, is a holy, GODly experience. We need to be open to experience our GOD in the silence, quietness, and gentleness of the moon-beam.

God is calling us to be in a unique oneness with 'Him'!

Calling us to be special, yet an integral part of all humankind, and

calling us to be totally human within

God's loving embrace!

That's GOD's REAL Love for each of us uniquely and together.

GOD Can't Be Found in the Computer Screen, Even Less in the SmartPhone – Just Look, Skyward!

As I looked skywards, for the first time in a long time, while sitting on the seashore on a bright full moon evening, it dawned very clearly on me that GOD is so much more than can be found on a computer screen or in a smartphone, as seen in the digital world, found locked up in cyberspace.

We cannot 'lock GOD up'. This is what the digital age seems to be trying to do, whether deliberately or otherwise.

I realised while looking towards the sky this evening, seeing the three levels of cloud, seeing the moon in all its glory on this full moon evening, seeing the awesomeness of celestial nature at her best, that our concentration on that small computer or mobile phone screen, etc., on a blinkered electronic reality, appears to diminish the validity of the awesomeness of our GOD.

We may very much become unintentionally closed to this reality of GOD and then closed to GOD. This is way too dangerous to imagine. We NEED all the help we can get from God! Pray!!!

I believe that the computer screens of all sizes encourage shallower thinking in all their supposed 'magnificence' and 'factual knowledge' and 'AI'. Is this a small intellectualisation of the reality of GOD? Over time, we seem to consciously or subconsciously believe that the truth of containment, as espoused by, or through, the computer screens, is actually real! It is NOT! Small screens also help us think that little is the answer.

GOD is beyond massive and awesome! God is infinity and more!

Not only small thinking becomes somewhat the norm, but little imagining, small emotionalising, small acceptance of the inherent closeness of GOD, who is yet still way beyond our everyday actualities, becomes closed, becomes digitalised – becomes unreal. We can't allow GOD to get lost in the electronics!

Imagine an existence where our imagination becomes locked inside a computer, or locked inside our brain, which believes the digitalised world is real, hence becoming for all intent and purpose, and believed existence inside a computer - becomes digitalised, i.e., becomes another worldly computer?

Yet still very real for the viewer of that computer screen.

Even greater disbelief for someone within the real world would be seeing someone who is locked, by virtue of that person's cyber-world reality, away from any real human emotion. That person is becoming more computer-emotional as the years progress.

It is becoming more - one emotionally with the digital world and less than one with the human world!

Wonderful human experiences within the real natural world and GOD can inspire anyone, even one within the emotionally and intellectually fraught cyber-world closed in realism, to see the reality of an extraordinary GOD within our human existence.

More moonbeams and sunbeams are needed to figuratively shine on to the computer screen to awaken the reality of the one behind these beams. The moonbeam's softness and the sunbeam's strength see our GOD in right action within this world always.

Music and Song - Fantastic Inspiration for True Love

Leo Downey and Leonard Cohen (deceased) – Contemporary Musicians for GOD and GOD's people

Karen and I often reflect on two unique musicians who have had a most incredible impact on our lives.

The talents of these two gentlemen go well beyond music and into the GODly realms. They are both very accomplished musicians in their own right.

Leonard Cohen (deceased) and Leo Downey are both now from Canada. These are our two most preferred musicians these days. Their musical talent is only surpassed by their commitment to GOD and their willingness to share their beliefs, thoughts, and feelings about many things spiritual and religious, along with their lifestyles, priorities, etc.

Their contemporary music inspires on several levels. Mostly, the loving relationship with GOD and fellow people is an integral aspect of each man's music and songs.

Leonard Cohen began the impact on Karen and me around ten years ago. My last 'Night of Excellence' introductory prayer segment at Aquinas College in 2009, as APRE at Aquinas, had Leonard's 'Hallelujah' as its main song and theme. Its impact on the audience was substantial.

Following is Leo Downey's unique music analysis highlighting his writing skills in his most reflective book, *Soultracker – Following Beauty*.

Leo Downey

We discovered Leo Downey's incredible musical talents and deep Marian spirituality five years ago in 2016 when visiting Canada. Staying at Leo's 'Rocky Mountain' Buffalo Ranch' in spectacular Golden in the Rocky Mountains, Canada, was astonishing. What brilliant scenery, fauna, and flora! Every corner of the road has a breathtaking WOW experience before you.

Music and songs written and performed by those close to GOD have a most remarkable impact on so many people searching for GOD. Leo's and Leonard's styles are outstandingly different from most religious recordings.

Leo had a rock band in California a few years back, and he still loves to write rock songs. His next album out soon will be a mixture of rock and love songs with lots of lead guitar. Highlighting Leo's superb guitar skills will be worth every moment.

Leo Downey is many things, primarily his deep spirituality with a massive commitment to GOD. His spirituality and religious beliefs are seen in many of his brilliant songs and his book - *Soultracker – Following Beauty*. Leo is truly one of Canada's best-kept secrets. His distinctive voice and brilliant guitar playing, combined with exceptional lyrics in his songs and reflective passages in his book, call out for others to explore his talent and closeness with GOD. I have found GOD in many of his songs, as well. (See Leo's website for Bio, music, and literary details - and so much more.

(http://leodowney.com/discography/leo-downey-2008/

http://leodowney.com/about-leo/)

Leo Downey, presently from Golden BC in the Canadian Rockies and formerly from California, USA, is a very talented and spiritual man. Leo also runs his buffalo (bison) ranch 'Rocky Mountain Buffalo Ranch' linked to his Air B&B log cabin on his most spectacular property surrounded by some of the most outstanding local Rockies' scenery imaginable. Leo is not only these exceptional musical and lifestyle realities but also a most accomplished author, having written *Soultracker – Following Beauty* with his follow-up books planned.

Having been fortunate to have met Leo while staying in his cabin was one of life's most inspirational moments for me. Karen, my wife, and our son, Andrew, and daughter-in-law, Shannon, stopped on our way back from Banff. I am also so glad I purchased his self-titled CD, *Leo Downey*. All his publications and reviews can be found on his webpage.

Leo intermingles his spiritual/religious songs with his everyday songs. The lyrics and music of these unique songs are gripping and inspirational. Leo's classic song is his *The Tears of Mary* with Leo and Karen Hansen Downey's words. Interestingly, we found quite a few mini statues of Mary throughout the cabin during our stay.

The Tears of Mary

Words by Leo Downey and Karen Hansen Downey, music by Leo Downey 1995

Pregnant with the future, pregnant with the past
Pregnant with the promised Child, that will take us home at last
Her heart becomes a meadow, her soul becomes a sea
Her Child is her creator, I believe the Mystery

The tears of Mary, are falling in GOD's eyes
Heaven kneels with a Mother and Child
The truth can be so simple, so innocent and holy
Laying in his mother's arms, a King in all his glory
The tears of Mary, are falling in GOD's eyes
Heaven kneels with a Mother and Child
You and I were born in the manger
Wise men came with a star
All this time, we have lived to remember
Just how holy we are
The tears of Mary, are falling in GOD's eyes
Heaven kneels with a Mother and Child

(*The Tears of Mary* by Leo Downey and Karen Hansen Downey)

Leo has this beautiful approach with his songs. The spiritual/religious songs don't sound like standard religious hymns but are very much contemporary, even though recorded a decade or so ago. His strong, talented voice and music are exemplified in *The Rest of My Life* - one such song. The most powerful lyrics end the song. There is a strong reference to Mary's virgin birth, as in *The Tears of Mary* song above.

The Rest of my Life (Extract)

Out of the west, a Pacific swell
Waves of grace curled and fell
The people were blessed, with the soul/song of the Earth
They started again, with a virgin birth

Bryan Foster

(The Rest of My Life by Leo Downey*)*

GOD's Little One tells a beautiful narrative about a newborn son's first year on earth. The poetic lyrics lift this song to another level once again. His unique style shows Leo's talent in being able to story-tell some beautiful life and religious lessons and experiences in an authentic, spiritualistic, GOD-loving way.

GOD's Little One

GOD gave us a home where the buffalo roam
Where the blueberries grow and so can our son
The first time I saw him all wrinkled and red
From a pool in the desert, mom and I said
Your first time around the sun
The Lord helped us raise you
Your first time around the sun
My little, our little, GOD's little One
You were raised in a time, when the world needs a sign
And her love has blown cold, but I'll warm you with mine
REP
Go run with the birds and the bees
Wherever they lead you
Wherever the buffalo roam
They will lead you, they will lead you,
They will lead you home
SOLO
REP
Must listen to songs include the following three from each very accomplished performer and mystic:

Leonard Cohen's: 'Anthem', 'Hallelujah' and 'Come Healing'.

Leo Downey's: 'Tears of Mary', 'GOD's Little One' and 'The Rest of My Life".

Two video songs definitely worth watching are: Leonard's 'Hallelujah'
at https://www.youtube.com/watch?v=YrLk4vdY28Q

And Leo's 'The Rest of My Life' – particularly check out his spirituality, the scenery, and buffalos/bison…
at https://www.youtube.com/watch?v=dS-OblC7c9M

We also include the 'Rocky Mountain Buffalo Ranch' video we made - for the scenery and feel of the Golden area in Canada's Rockies. Leo and his buffalos, cabins and majestic backdrops + waterfalls, wolves, and a grizzly bear feature at https://www.youtube.com/watch?v=UCdA2UN5KqA

(*GOD's Little One* by Leo Downey)

Printed with written permission from Leo Downey, Golden, Canada.

http://leodowney.com/discography/leo-downey-2008/

http://leodowney.com/about-leo/

The Risen Christ and the Risen Sun - Easter

Each morning the sun rises. Each morning the resurrected Christ is there for us all. The rising sun is a warm reminder of GOD's unique presence for us in the Eucharist and our everyday lives.

Easter is the most glorious time for Christians, followers of Christ, the resurrected incarnate GOD. It is time to celebrate GOD's defeat of death and evil.

The rising sun follows the dark of the night — metaphorically, the glorified sun rises to eternal salvation from the darkened tombs.

Like many of us, do you see the rising sun when the priest slowly raises the host at the consecration? Is the sun being a metaphor for the host, i.e., God?

The sun is the nearest massive power source we have, which we can observe. It is the only one for us.

It more than represents our 1 GOD of this world. It gives light to our world. It gives life to our world. Without the sun, we are nothing; we die, we don't exist.

Without GOD, we have no light, no life, just eternal death, and damnation.

Easter celebrates the light of GOD in this world. Let's all celebrate what this should mean for every human. The light source becomes especially present for Christians on the Easter weekend. All people, no matter their religion or personal beliefs, are one with GOD. There is only ONE GOD for eternity for all genuine religions. A most freeing experience once understood.

GOD rose for us. Let us rise to Easter's challenge for our one and only GOD of all religions and beliefs forever!

A Loving GOD – as Seen Through Two Perspectives

There is a GOD - as billions of people can attest to this reality, over thousands of years. There are so many ways to explain this answer. However, in a widely secular, materialistic, individualistic world, the challenge is even more significant. I will approach the response from the following two perspectives: 1. Faith, and 2. Historical, Cultural, Lived perspectives.

1. Faith

Faith experiences throughout the world are considerable. There is no doubt that billions of people believe in GOD out of faith. This belief may or may not have other experiences attached. They just know and feel that it is an actual divine presence. They know that this helps them in their lives to live fulfilling and substantial lives for themselves and others. They feel the support and presence of GOD in their lives. They interact with GOD through prayer and within the living world created by GOD and cared for by them.

I find it very difficult to see why this is such a significant challenge for doubters. If there is a GOD, then surely this divine 'world' of GOD is different from our physical world. How we of the physical world interact with the divine world/GOD would be by definition quite different.

This could explain why so many have faith instead of a scientific explanation of the divine or GOD. Science is of the physical world. GOD is of the heavenly world. People use science to help explain the physical world. People mainly use faith and their spiritual/religious experiences to present and interact with the divine world in rather limited terms, concepts, and ways.

But they know GOD the divine is real!

Science is GOD's gift to humanity to help us make sense of everything physical created by GOD. It begins the understanding of GOD's discovery. Science and faith can work together to help us find and considerably appreciate our GOD and GOD's relationship with us and this world.

However, Science may be interested in exploring why 'tears of love' exist. 'Tears from GOD' often accompany intimate religious experiences with GOD through prayer, relationships and nature, etc. A physical sign of GOD's presence is through these 'tears of Love'/"Tears from GOD'!

2. Historical, Cultural, Lived

Various cultures have lived their beliefs for thousands of years and still do. In some cultures, it is the extreme case not to believe in GOD or the divine. In themselves, these two points, Faith and the Historical offer a strong case for a belief in GOD and divinity!

For those who say that people believe out of habit or need something to believe in, or fear death and the afterlife, there may be some justification for this. However, this does not allow for a mature faith where a person accepts the beliefs as an adult and leaves the childish, blind beliefs behind. These people are true adult believers and once again welcome the wondrous divine through limited human experience, discoveries, and all the difficulties this entails.

There is One GOD

Found by the Author Through a 25th Birthday Spiritual Experience

There is GOD! There are so many ways to explain this statement. However, in a widely secular, materialistic, individualistic world, the challenge is even more significant. I will approach the answer from the personal experience perspective.

GOD is absolute Love. Love is the meaning of life. GOD's Love is the meaning of life.

When you experience GOD in such an authentic, loving way that your life is forever changed for the good, you rarely ever doubt the existence of GOD again, and you live a very much changed lifestyle. Turn the hurt and harm over to God as much as you can.

I experienced GOD in a unique experience on my 25th birthday. I was not a charismatic Catholic or born-again Christian; in fact, I actually fought against what I perceived might happen to me if I allowed a religious sister to pray over me. I couldn't resist the experience any longer and was prayed over after a unique school Eucharistic celebration. My whole body started to be filled with a most incredible warming experience, beginning at the top of my head where sister's hands were laid and moving down through my body until it reached my feet. It felt as if my old self was being washed out, and I was being filled with this most loving feeling.

At once, I began to experience tears, uncontrollably - Tears of God. Absolute love for and from GOD, who now became as

177

apparent as anything else that is real, which I have ever experienced, were forthcoming. Almost 40 years later, my recollection is as if I had a video of the experience. Tears of Love well in the eyes or crying occur whenever I closely experience the love of GOD. It happened at the birth of each of my children. It occurs when an extra special beautiful thing happens in the world of nature or with people. It happens whenever I retell my stories of love. It happens somewhat regularly when living close to God, family, and friends.

These events may be extremely simple everyday happenings or may be quite complicated. All these events have GOD present. The GOD of LOVE! These experiences involve the physical – 'Tears from God'.

Yes, this is quite raw emotion and nothing for which to apologise. The loving emotion is the window to GOD. GOD gives believers ways to know GOD is here. The tearful and crying experiences can be quantitative. These are not just faith experiences. These are real, different from every day crying tears, and are from GOD.

(See more detail in Appendix 1.)

> Yes, this is quite raw emotion and nothing for which to apologise.
>
> The loving emotion is the window to God.
>
> God gives the believers ways to know God is here.

GOD Loves – in 'No Man's Land'

The final sentence from Roland Fishman's, 2014, *No Man's Land* was divinely inspired.

A unique encounter with GOD - through the last sentence of a thriller novel - set on New Year's Eve.

Having not read a novel for a few years, I was drawn to this novel by Karen, my wife, who swapped for it while camping at Suffolk Park caravan park, near Byron Bay, Australia. She thoroughly enjoyed it and strongly encouraged me to read it.

It was destined to be intensely inspirational. It started and concluded in the surf at Lennox Heads, Australia, just down from Byron Bay, coincidentally for us. Its conclusion, as well as a critical event in the story, revolved around huge waves - both the brilliance of catching an enormous wave's barrel, as well as almost drowning when held under by massive water forces. I have been very 'fortunate' to have experienced similar myself and survived to tell. Each has been life-changing! The storyline moves to both Mullumbimby and Boggabilla, places I have also frequented, as well as an international destination and an Australian state capital, Sydney.

The book contained some key spirituality points, nothing more so than the novel's last line, literally.

"For some reason unknown to him, a reason that had nothing to do with Islam, Christianity or any other religion he… whispered, 'Allah Akbar [GOD is the greatest]."

To me, once again, this pointed to the existence of only 1 GOD for all people - ever! And it occurred in a fiction novel. How good is this?

As I read the last sentence, the Tears from GOD flowed!

Once again, GOD told me that there is only 1 GOD for the whole universe in a different genre – a novel. There is only One GOD – ever! And that there is no one single religion (yet!). All genuine religions have a crucial role in getting this new GOD message today to their people. This is primarily for the two religions directly concerned with the Incarnation from the 21 Revelations from God to Bryan in 2016 and 2018 – Christianity and Islam. Yet a massive change religiously is needed, as there is only a need for One, True religion when all genuine religions combine as this ONE!

What would it take for this to occur? Will it probably need a unique experience or appearance of God in our world? It would need to be an outstanding event or Godly appearance, etc., along with people able to change to a One God Only belief. It would probably take many years actually to occur, if at all?

The last line, written in Roland Fishman's novel, is in the text box following. One God Only is referred to here as Allah, Islam's name for GOD. This is as happens throughout many of the sacred scriptures from many of the authentic religions worldwide.

Allah, God, Yahweh, Brahma/n, etc., are titles of a single God for each of these religions. There are enough pointers, though, to there being Only One God forever, for this to be accepted here. Even though each religion virtually denies each other's God as their God, there is enough evidence scripturally, as well as in the 21 Revelations from GOD to this *Series'* Book 6's author in 2016 and 2018, for this One God to be true.

What do you think?

Quote: Roland Fishman, 2014, *No Man's Land,* Rising Tide Books, Sydney – p. 367. See website for details: http://www.rolandfishman.com.au/

"For some reason unknown to him,

a reason that had nothing to do with

Islam, Christianity or any other religion he…
whispered,

'Allah Akbar [God is the greatest].'"

Roland Fishman

There is only one GOD – forever!

And that there is no one single religion (yet)!

All genuine religions have a crucial role in getting
this new message of GOD today to their people.

Ideally, a massive change religiously is needed as
there is only a Need for One, True religion.

All genuine religions need to combine, in time,

as this – ONE RELIGION FOR ALL!

By Book 6's Author

Bryan Foster

Marian Valley, Queensland – the GOD Experiences of my Wife, Karen, and me – Do You Have a Special Place?

Karen and I both experienced remarkable 'Tears from GOD' moments during a recent Sunday mass at Marian Valley, 10km from Canungra, Queensland, Australia. These occurred numerous times throughout the mass in the Black Madonna Chapel.

For Karen, these mainly occurred during the Eucharistic Prayer beginning with the Holy Holy Holy sung in Latin and the use of the traditional incense and concluded with the Our Father. While for me, it was a little more specific during the consecration. The readings beautifully prepared the congregation through the highlighted themes of Love, Repentance, and Forgiveness.

Both of us experienced one of the most profound experiences of encountering GOD within the Eucharist. These moments truly brought us into close contact with GOD we hadn't experienced at this level at Mass before. We could feel the true presence of GOD with and in us!

This encounter with the one and only GOD of the universe, followed by all legitimate religions that follow GOD, came for me after many days of relaxing back into nature. Camping beside a stream in Canungra and driving the country roads to the Stinson plane wreck brought a real closeness with the local flora and fauna.

I write this encounter on Fatima Day, which is currently being celebrated with a Mass at Marian Valley. This morning I also had a fascinating chat with a married couple of Seven Day Adventist followers beachside at Surfers Paradise while on my bike ride. Interestingly, this was the day before they left for a new posting in southern central NSW and a year since our chance encounter at Point Lookout. Coincidence or pre-destination...?

Details about Marian Valley are available from their website + Facebook page:

Order of St Paul the First Hermit
10km from Canungra and 28km from Nerang on Beechmont Road
Shrine of Our Lady Help of Christians
Main Chapel seats 500 and is known as the Black Madonna Chapel
http://marianvalley.org.au/
https://www.facebook.com/MarianValleyShrine/

Notes attached to Sunday's Readings at Marian Valley, Qld, Australia:

We have a moral obligation to correct blatant wrongdoing, whether in the family, the workplace, or society. But it is incumbent on those who have others in their care to offer correction with love and respect. The old dictum, "hate the sin but love the sinner," is a good guideline in many situations, as is St Paul's principle: "Owe no one anything, except to love one another."

(http://marianvalley.org.au/)

https://www.associationofcatholicpriests.ie/

The Love of Priests and Pastors for their Communities

Listening to both the Gospel of Jesus being baptized by John the Baptist and the accompanying Homily by Fr Jason Middleton today, highlighted for me once again the love of the priests and pastors for their flocks. Unfortunately, a loving relationship is often misunderstood, or deliberately ignored, or actively fought against, in today's world!

Far too much negative publicity and media attention have been given to the relatively few priests who have been involved in horrific acts with minors throughout the world. It is very understandable why this negativity has happened, and it is not to be ignored, but learned from, particularly due to the high standing of priests within society. Now is the time to place this in its actual perspective. Significantly few priests statistically have been involved. The statistic is less for priests than for men in general in society (<1% for clergy, compared to 2.5%, which is the accepted research statistic these days for non-clergy males).

When supporting or criticising the Catholic Church, we must remember that the Church employs the second largest number of people in the nation after public servants in Australia's public services.

The Christian church institution is a significant example of good in today's world and has been for over 2000 years. Unfortunately, so many evil people these days are trying to eliminate the church from our world. These evil people blame the church for all of society's and the church's wrongs. They have no legitimate appreciation of what they are accusing good, decent, honourable priests, in particular, about! Significantly harmful is their 'blanket blame on all priests'. It seems the priests are legitimate targets in the evil people's minds. The scamming members of the open society also litigate against the church for their own financial gain, claiming any amount of lies to justify their claim. It appears that the rule of law becomes a bit weaker when it regularly finds 'innocent priests guilty' because of the often uncontested views of a supposed victim. However, we must never forget that a low percentage of priests did evil acts and should be moved on from the church and serve time in jail when guilty. These days the great majority of guilty priests are no longer priests, many are in prison. Hopefully, very few priests were found guilty when innocent.

Where have been the positive stories that abound? The great, great majority of priests have lovingly gone about their pastoral, sacramental and administrative lives in ways which genuinely benefit their communities and society. This is often in difficult and sometimes hostile circumstances. Not only do these good, innocent men have to bear the brunt of an ill-informed or unforgiving public regarding abuse, they are also often accused or considered guilty by association – purely because they are priests. This is an evil action by these people against innocent priests. Just as the actual numbers of pedophiles among non-priests are relatively low, so it is with the priests – yet relatively lower.

Very few will deny that justice of the guilty must be seen to be done. Society must now accept that this is being done - because it is – from the top (Pope), down in the Church!

Society needs to move onwards to allow the other innocent men to be themselves, free of all associated guilt, etc.

Yes, we all seem to know of various priests and pastors who don't fit our expectations of their vocation, but yet do nothing illegal or unethical. Still, out of love from GOD for these dedicated people, we need to allow for legal and ethical differences and meet them where they are – we may even be able to gently change them in ways which suit both them and ourselves if this is needed.

I have been deeply involved with the Catholic Church and Catholic schools for my whole life – over 60 years. My wife and I were both Catholic teachers. I have now resigned from teaching religion to high school students and concentrate on my writings of religious books. Karen thoroughly enjoys still teaching year 2. We have three children, two of whom also teach in Catholic schools. In my time, I have only known of priests and pastors who want to do what is best for their communities. I am aware that there will be some who would say that I am biased (yet I could add - no more biased than anyone else who supports the Truth and follows the Truth given by God). Yet to live within the Church for so long allows for a more complete understanding of the real situation. This is no rose-tinted appreciation – it is honestly real.

As for any person, priests or pastors are no different when it comes to highs and lows. There have been times when a priest or pastor's behaviour or personality may not have suited me when they seemed hostile or aggressive. Yet, I now realise with age and experience that an understanding and acceptance is very much needed. Priests are religious gentlemen and ladies for GOD.

A priest is a person and priesthood is his/her vocation. Likewise, for pastors - firstly, they are people and secondly their vocation is one of being a pastor.

As an example, a few years back, Fr Peter Dillon, my PP and Dean of the local Deanery, along with Fr Jason Middleton, Associate Pastor, of my parish, the Southport Catholic Parish on the Gold Coast, Australia, are mighty men who lovingly give their lives to

GOD and GOD's people. Fr Peter is my age. His first associate pastor role was in the parish where my first teaching position was. We met there. Fr Jason was ordained a few years ago. Quite a gap, yet both are very passionate about supporting their parishioners in whatever ways are required. Absolutely, no hint of anything illegal or immoral for me over the years from these priests (or any others!).

I believe that these men are quite typical of our priests today, as we settle down after the crisis, which we have just been exploring in this chapter. They are heavily involved within their parish, e.g. at both the primary and secondary Catholic schools in their parish; the aged care facilities in the parish grounds; the local public and private hospitals and other welfare agencies; visitations to parishioners; the celebration of the sacraments in three different churches; etc. – quite a load for just two men – and I don't even know the full extent of other activities and involvements of these generous men.

The love of priests and pastors for their communities is real!

There is so much in this mainly selfless love from which we can all gain. Once we accept these people for who they are, firstly as people and secondly as priests/pastors, we will be appreciative of our similarities and differences and work together to better our society as a whole.

Those who thrive on 'cheap shots' against priests, church, Islam, imams, God, etc., unfortunately, will pay the price that God decides, unless they authentically are sorry for their evil and confrontational comments, seek forgiveness from God and anyone harmed and try and make restitution to those they hurt through their hostile verbal or written attacks or physical harm. Just because you may have some thoughts about GOD's nonexistence, it doesn't matter, because GOD is real, does exist, and wants the best from and for all people. This is not a debate. There are profound Truths from GOD, which humanity and individuals must accept. It is not a game! It is real! No-one can change this Truth, whatever their personal views.

GOD's Absolute Love of all people is also aimed at those evil people who hate love, peace, compassion, etc. GOD wants these people to be genuinely forgiven for their sins. It is all up to the evil ones to turn to God and authentically request forgiveness and turn away from evil. If they can't, then that is their decision to end up existing in what they like best, as shown through their earthly behaviour, i.e. evil. Hell awaits them if they seriously accept evil as superior to Good. If they accept hate as being superior to Love.

It is all up to the evil ones to turn to God and authentically request forgiveness and turn away from evil.

If they can't,

then that is their decision to end up existing in what they like best,

as shown through their earthly behaviour,

i.e. evil.

Hell awaits them if they seriously accept evil as superior to Good. If they accept hate as being superior to Love.

I have been deeply involved with the Catholic Church and Catholic schools for my whole life – over 60 years. My wife and two of our children are Catholic teachers. I was also for 42 years, until retiring from teaching. Now I am writing religious and caravan/trailer travel books.

In my time, I have only known of priests, pastors and religious brothers and sisters, who want to do what is best for their communities. Nothing illegal or unethical.

I am aware that there will be some who would say that I am biased (yet I would add - no more biased than anyone else who supports the Truth and follows the Truth given by God).

Yet, for me to live within the Church for so long, allows for a more complete understanding of the real situation.

This is no rose-tinted appreciation – it is honestly real.

Bryan Foster

Priests and Pastors – Don't Ignore GOD's Messengers

I personally have tears from GOD and of sorrow and sadness as I check out my various Facebook friends who are priests of this magnificent Church. As 'Tears of Mary' by Leo H. Downey is playing in the background.

Why are so few people openly following, watching, wanting God or the institutional religions in their lives...??? Is this a demographic thing?

I still feel relatively young, yet I feel so old viewing the church attendees and most of the clergy. The young priests are extra special in that they have to help carry the misbehaviour various more senior priests have done worldwide – mainly paedophilia.

The extraordinary young teachers at our Catholic or other religious schools and elsewhere, who are drawn through their love of GOD to the beautiful and loving institution of the Church, are so inspiring.

How much of a challenge must it be for our magnificent young men who are priests today? They must cop all the reactions from so many observers and followers of the Royal Commission into paedophilia, even though their generation had nothing or very little to do with paedophilia. Unfortunately, they must wear it and then espouse homilies of the TRUE beauty and wonder of Christ/GOD.

I met Leo Downey, a lover of Christ and his mother Mary, in a most isolated and stunning part of Canada a few years ago. He is a most brilliant musician and mystical writer who sings and writes about his love of GOD and Mary the Mother of Jesus.

The cottage I stayed in had small figurines of Mary and crosses scattered throughout this farm in isolated Golden in BC, Canada. Leo, just younger than me, lives in his self-made smallish two-story timber cottage adjacent to where we stayed. Buffalos (bison) shared the property. Brilliant backdrops of snow-capped Rocky Mountains with pine trees abounding and turquoise waterfalls were nearby. GOD was truly present – EVERYWHERE!

If only more young people, along with the broad demographic between the young teachers to whom I referred and Leo's and my generation, could see the wonder of GOD in this world. See it through our young priests, teachers, other good decent people, spectacular environments throughout the world, holy natural or humanmade places etc. everywhere.

Our One GOD of the universe is there for everyone. Let our priests and pastors know we support, love and dedicate ourselves to them and their lifelong love journey in GOD. Their leadership is essential for the magnificent Christian Church, especially the vast Catholic Church of the contemporary world.

Our One God of the Universe is there for

EVERYONE - FOREVER.

RELIGIOUS LOVE CHALLENGES TODAY

Introduction for Religious Love Challenges

One approach says that there are several religious challenges when considering *Love is the Meaning of Life: God's Love*. The difficulty with this topic and theme is the need to appreciate the meaning of some of the critical terms before a more complete understanding can be reached. 'Love' in this book concentrates mainly on the Divine, GODLY Love of AGAPE and how this unconditional LOVE impacts the reader when considering each term's essential meanings in the book's title.

Agape love is where you wish to share your love without expecting anything in return, no strings attached. God's Love is precisely this – Agape Love. Our love for God should also be this type. According to many religious commentators, scriptural scholars, and theologians, it is the highest form of love. The next level is when considering the genuine and authentic physical, passionate love between two human lovers.

Social justice and human rights principles have some basic and complex definitions and ways of being practised and implemented. The ability to love yourself and love others is implicit for this type of Love. Even though the physical appearance is one of the attractive features humans display and share, it is not essential. Still, it could become critical to those lacking in an appreciation of Agape, unconditional love.

Some religious challenges for the religious leaders also include the successful use of social networking websites, the cynical rejection of God by atheists, the negative impact of secularism in our world, the role of subjects like religious education in schools, and the mostly silent media on religious topics, especially God, forgiveness and all other aspects of Godly Love.

Bryan Foster

A relatively new religious challenge could be considered as bullying. The Holy Churches, different religions and denominations, and their congregation/people often complain about how they are treated by society or community members. As time goes on, the non-religious populations, continue to grow and then in many instances pressurise the believers and followers of GOD. The bullying is based upon these bullies being: evil, haters, heretics who then cause believers, outward or silent types, and others, to be in genuine fear of being a religious follower.

I recently tried an experiment, whereby I noted many of my key points from Book 3 and Book 5. I placed these on two Facebook titles for what I thought were 1) supportive or 2) not supportive of my religious beliefs. The supportive page was better than the other but did become quite harsh over time. These people sounded as if they were being bullied somewhere and were going to take it out on me! However, I also wondered if they weren't supporters at all, but hate-filled individuals, doing their best to discredit the author, etc. The not supportive page was aptly titled and filled with hate, anger, disbelief, atheism, etc.

Most students of 'Love' people would list around eight types of Love. The first four, are summarised here. The first most often used is Agape – God-like and perfect. The selfless, unconditional kind of Love. GOD's love for each of us equally. The second most-often used type is Erotic Love – the physical and romantic kind between two people in love. Followed by the third type being Eros – this is the married state of deep love and fertility. Children are a part of this group. The fourth type of love is Philia or friendship. These are the daily relationships between the people within your life.

Social Justice Principles and Human Rights

In Christianity for well over two thousand years, social justice principles became the major lifestyle and workers' principles of equality from the 19th century during the Industrial Revolution, as people in Europe aimed to become egalitarian societies. These principles are now also being taught as 'Human Rights' principles by a secular world, since becoming UN statutes from 1948 after World War II. These are part of the world's governments' plans, through the United Nations, to never allow the horrors of war to occur again. However, this is very important for the religious and secular worlds. If these principles had remained only as Church teachings, their importance wouldn't reach or affect most of the world's population today. The continual present-day denial of so much of the traditional and religious world order, based on the religious, social justice principles, along with the Human Rights from relatively a short time ago, shows that today's world overall, did not learn much from history and religious traditions and by its actions or inactions will potentially take itself into the abyss unless corrected quickly.

The intellectuals and middle to upper classes have no right to demean those less fortunate. These privileged groups are often repositioning the moral values of others inconsiderately. The wealthy and educated have no right to force their moral values on to the poor. Respect for the values of the poor is critical. Yet, the world should be trying to bring equality to all people, especially the disadvantaged and poor in so many ways.

Often, the wealthy's belief that the poor control their lives is misguided and very wrong. The less fortunates' problems can rarely be solved with the wealthy's unfair solutions. Living in harsh conditions, with little income or reserves, minimal educational and career opportunities, and few or any 'contacts', needs a unique appreciation to attain improvement. Helping the poor, with respect for each person to solve their problems, would be more successful. This would require the non-poor to be open to the poor's messages, which will invariably be based on sharing and equality.

Social justice has been so-called and operative within the Christian religions, especially in Catholicism, since the early 19th century, where it became a significant part of the Catholic social teachings. These principles are at the heart and centre of Christianity. They are the basis of all the teachings of Jesus, Moses, Mahammad and various other historical religious leaders through the past 4-5000 years or so? ('Mahomad' was spelt this way in Revelation #15 from God to Bryan in 2016.)

Human Rights began after World War 2 in the secular world. The United Nations adopted these in 1948. This Universal Declaration of Human Rights states what the freedoms and rights of every person equally throughout the world. Placing these side-by-side with the social justice principles shows the enormous similarity of both sets. The UN showed how accurate both these sets of principles are for all cultures, genuine religions, countries, etc.

The world is becoming more secular, self-centred and critical of most beliefs beyond each person's views. A selfish, greedy, inconsiderate, materialistic world is slowly emerging as the norm. Communities of all sorts within society as a whole, need to support and promote all the social justice principles and human rights vigorously, wherever the opportunities arise. This is mostly due to many of these principles being lost within the world's greed and selfishness.

See Bibliography for domains' details:

Catholic Social Teaching for Best Practice
The Origins of Social Justice…
What are human rights?

Bryan Foster

Perfection – Being Physically Perfect! Why? Where's the Genuine Love?

Why do people try so much to be perfect? Especially in the physical appearance stakes. There is nothing wrong with people aiming to be the best possible, as long as it doesn't change the person and who they authentically are. Yet we need to realise that this is never perfect. To accept whatever happens to be the best at that particular moment or period is necessary. During this initial consideration of the plan, the best reaction maybe, "Don't do it!"

The problem arises while aiming for perfection to become way too passionate about the expected result. To possibly become so excessive in the attempts being made and the desired outcome, the aimed-for results, never being perfect, are doing psychological harm. In this Instagram/Facebook/Twitter/etc. world, the young in particular are using so many apps/software at their disposal, to 'create' who they want to be and pretend that this is who they are. 'Photoshopping' becomes so needed that the person is often unrecognisable or becomes strangely different in the finished image. Nothing but perceived perception eventuates. Disappointingly.

Then we have all the body surgery operations available to change our appearance if we so choose. Again often to be unrecognisable. Some of the work being done on people makes them often look fake or a strangely reprofiled human. Many seem to thrive with this unnatural appearance, often because their social group is doing likewise. Each person within their group supports the others too often to excessive lengths, often unreasonably, given their changed appearance. This may lead to exaggerated pumped up (duck) lips, the way too-large, large 'solid' breasts, and the failure to accept reality and what is best for each person. All these and more can have exaggerated, unreal, finished products often on an unsuspecting lady! Men's physical beauty changes are increasing considerably in number these recent years.

In many cases, male or female, there is so much that has changed for these people physically that their self-esteem and self-worth either take a hammering after they evaluate the surgery, the finished product, or the look screams out that this person is having real psychological or sociological problems. Yet in some cases, the appearance seems to be reasonably good. However, it is still the person who has changed their natural appearance. This appears to be challenged by some ethical and moral issues. It isn't now who they are 'inside' but who they portray on the outside. (Is this what a successful, hard-working, every day, loving person needs?) It is the self-worth that helps with self-esteem - that is what needs to be essential for everyone.

Many could ask, what do I need to do for me to be the best loving person I can be? Who shows their love for all whenever possible. Who is genuinely me and not a fake physical shell of my true self?

It is quite disturbing to hear adolescent-aged students justifying their make-up being worn at school, and often used excessively, as essential for their self-esteem and hence must be allowed to be worn. This claim is sometimes extended to also causing mental health issues if they were stopped from wearing it at school. Is this an initial starting point for some of the whole physical appearance, which leads to the surgical process not much more along in their lives? I wonder how much of this is related to parents who automatically get their children's teeth straightened or adjusted in various ways by specialist dentists – primarily for the appearance. If dental work is needed for the right corrective, necessary reasons, this shouldn't be an issue. If their teeth, jaw or gums have significant problems and need adjustments, this is a fundamental reason for repairs. Perfect teeth are not a necessity; effective and practical ones are though. Unfortunately, specialist teeth work is expensive. You virtually need private health cover with extras to help with the costs these days.

Virtually, everyone knows that the pressure on various societal demographics is the backstory to so much of this problem. In several cases, it seems that new and old media are once again at the forefront. This is also dependant on the country or culture these people live in or from which they come.

The happier we all are with our GOD given personal physical appearance, the better our lives should be. Our personal, not perfect physical appearance should be the aim. This helps with the genuine love we offer to others and ourselves.

GOD doesn't make mistakes. We all look physically the way GOD wants us to look. Sometimes we ask, why? Other times we ask for improvements. Sometimes we may even, unfortunately, reject the divine plan for ourselves.

We have to act with integrity. We need to be our authentic selves for GOD. We need to NEED GOD! We need to ask GOD seriously, what 'He' wants from each of us, the way we are, not the way we may want to become. Genuineness is essential when relating to GOD. You are an individual, genuine, loving person. Successful in various ways. Helpful in other ways. If changes are wanted to improve ourselves, we should seek and act on those we need. We need to communicate with GOD about these issues, feelings, desires, etc. GOD will help you appreciate who you really are, why you are here on Earth and what GOD needs from and for you.

Social Networking Websites Critically Needed by Religions for the Word of GOD!

Churches can benefit from appropriate, creative, use of social media networking sites. Increasingly, this form of communication is becoming more evident for parishes. Be aware of all the privacy and legal issues as you work for this communication form to work for you!

The Challenge

Once again, we are challenged to meet our parishioners where they are or might be, shortly. The social networking tentacles are reaching further into the various demographics affecting our parish communities, often way beyond church leaders' awareness. No longer is it just the teens and '20 somethings', it is now common for people in their 50s, 60s and 70s to have one or more social networking accounts.

The Misconception

With respect, and only to make a point shout out loudly, the misconception is that this form of communication is just used for an inane chat amongst 'dizzy lightweights'!

Yes, this may be so for several users; however, there is a considerably large and ever-growing group of people who use this for much more than chat, even though legitimate discussion does play an essential part in many communication forms.

These people are not only building and strengthening relationships amongst friends and newly formed acquaintances/friends through their engagement online with each other and often doing so simultaneously, but they may also be adding depth to crucial aspects of their lives.

What are the Assumptions Underlying Social Networking Websites?

There are many exciting assumptions an ever-expanding group of people, with representatives in all age groups, of the 21st century, make:

• People like to build trusting relationships with others before doing 'business' (Churches need to be open to appreciating this belief and then adapting the way they communicate with such people. They want good people sharing valuable information.)
• The busyness of life often limits face-to-face opportunities
• The relationship does not need to be a face-to-face encounter, even though this is often preferred
• 'anonymity' allows for a less inhibited sharing of ideas and thoughts. It, therefore, also means it is somewhere to critique and then hide. (Easier for some people to make a comment when the contact person isn't actually in front of them. Similar to some people when using telephones or email.)
• The internet often provides the answers people seek (How often do you hear more and more, "Google it"?)
• Digital communication is the easiest and quickest means of communication and often the cheapest format too
• Digital communication allows for multiple conversations and digital communication simultaneously
• People using these forms of communication usually trust in the results due to their experiences.

Why Consider Social Networking Websites?

To reach this ever-growing majority group of people in our communities, we must meet them where they are at!

In many circumstances, this may not be your 'cup of tea'. But you do have control over who sees and comments on your church social networking pages if you follow the security directions. You may limit membership to only parishioners, and hence only these people and yourself will see what you and they say and show.

However, it is a successful method of informing an ever-growing group of your community of whatever it is you would like to inform them about.

The example below is the details contained on the Facebook page of the St Mary's Parish, Coomera, Australia and shows some ways a church parish uses this social networking site:

• Parish and Contact Details
• News from the Parish Priest and Responses from Parishioners
• News about Youth and Children's Activities and Responses
• Upcoming Parish Events
• Parish Photos
• Parish Priest Recommended Websites for Parishioners

Social networking sites can be used effectively by churches and parishes. Once many challenges, misconceptions and assumptions underlying social networking sites are initially explored, each parish will be able to decide whether to proceed with a social networking webpage. Those in doubt should search out experts in social media to gain a descent appreciation of these.

The Unwanted Negative Expert on GOD

I definitely don't have all the answers, yet I have been challenged by several people on Facebook who make strong statements as if they do have all the answers. And, that to know GOD or no God, is so easy! They believe that the answer is simple – it is what you 'believe'!? No cross-checking, prayer, GOD involvement, etc., needed. "I believe it!" is the statement. The assumption is that belief is all you need for it to be the Truth. No matter how false it may be.

Why do so many people believe that with a few 'search' clicks on Google or Bing or a couple of shared posts on Facebook or Instagram, or a quick Wiki read, that they are suddenly experts on GOD? Gathering from comments I have been receiving through various Facebook groups, it is becoming more apparent that people with little or no background in religion or GOD, suddenly feel entitled to offer the most outrageous views on GOD and GOD's teachings - as FACT! Or even use this to try and 'prove' GOD doesn't exist – which is impossible, as God is divine, not physical. GOD can't be proven as real or false by either the divine or physical experiences.

Of course, everyone is entitled to their viewpoint. Yet, this doesn't make it a correct fact or the Truth from GOD. To state these personal, uninformed beliefs as the Truth is akin to denying some strong scientific belief because you want to... e.g. the climate change deniers won't accept the substantial evidence of this widely accepted scientific belief and offer the alternative view as the fact. (We also cannot deny the variety and levels of various truths. Another discussion point.)

I accept that one of the premises of Book 1, *1GOD.world: One God for All* is to keep GOD's messages expressed in a simple to understand language so that these can be appreciated and lived out in ways applicable to all people. That is one of the essential principles of this *GOD Today Series*.

However, through appreciating this simplicity, it is not to be taken that everyone's views are correct and thrown around as the Truth – just because these may sound correct, for no particular reason.

There is only one Absolute Truth, and that is from GOD. We have no right to interpret it as we please. If this was the case, there is no Absolute Truth, apart from whatever you want it to be!

Through a combination of Revelation, inspiration and an informed education in GOD, religion, and various communities, there are correct ways to understand and appreciate GOD's teachings for us all. All forms of religious scripture, across the multiple faiths, need the necessary explanations and wisdom to gain the truth. There is far too much criticism of GOD and religion based on the minimal literal, fundamental appreciation of scriptures. The contextual approach is the majority accepted best way to appreciate scripture from GOD. Not the literal word.

The various genuine faiths worldwide usually have very high theological, scriptural and ethical education/training. This allows for a more proper interpretation of God's teachings and Revelations. From my many decades of experience with God's messages, the contextual approach allows for the best appreciation and interpretations of scripture and theology in all the scholarly methods used. The contextual approach is the message found within the scriptural or religious teachings when explored according to the context, language, era, community, politics, different religions' input and sometimes worldly events, etc. from when initially written. The fundamentalist approach often gets way too caught up within the literal, fundamental, scriptural interpretation. It ignores the contextual approach in general. Therefore, invariably misses the essential points being given by GOD to our communities.

The researcher needs to initially become very educated to be familiar with the various interpretative and analytical approaches, in particular, and to gain a better appreciation of the inspired and revealed Word of GOD. (This is a vast body of knowledge and wisdom compiled and regularly added to over centuries and sometimes over the millennia. It also comprises many more aspects of exploration, needing thorough consideration.)

From these findings, informed people must explain GOD's messages clearly and concisely, and as thoroughly as possible, without losing any context or content.

More so, it is the duty of the correctly informed, once at peace with their knowledge and appreciation of GOD's messages, to impart this to the population.

Beware the uninformed, ill-advised, often strong evil characters who force their untruths upon the world. Be even more aware of the evil ones trying very hard to make mischief but much worse, trying to corrupt GOD's Truth and even erode the belief of GOD in our world.

Atheists, i.e. non-believers of GOD, are extremely dangerous, not wanting the Truth from GOD or GOD to be accepted by anyone. No belief in GOD can only lead to -

No GOD = World Chaos

No GOD = Ethical Chaos

GOOD becomes Bad often quite quickly, as most people will do what they want for themselves while here on Earth. Their belief is that: "No-one cares about me, so why should I care about anyone else?" So false! Yet so enticing for these sorts of non-believers.

Therefore if there is No GOD for observing their misbehaviour - Bad Behaviour from many will result. Greed and non-Truths will permeate the religious and personal beliefs worldwide.

It is time for those who believe otherwise with little background understanding, or who are searching for a yet to be found GOD, to search in the right quarters, become far better informed, and accept that a certain depth of education is necessary for appreciating anything of substance, particularly when about the ultimate Truth, GOD.

There is Only One Absolute Truth,

and that is, and from, GOD.

We have no right to interpret Truth as we please.

If this was the case, then there is no Absolute Truth, apart from whatever you want it to be! There is far too much criticism of GOD

and religion based on the minimal literal appreciation of scriptures.

The Contextual Approach to scriptural interpretation is essential to gain GOD's Absolute Truth Today.

Bryan Foster

The 30% Who say 'No Religion', Do Not Necessarily Believe it Equals 30% atheists

Using a whole of the country census, Australia's 2016 one as an example, who could be blamed for thinking or believing that -

GOD is dead! (?)

GOD is dying! (?)

GOD never was! (?) Many could accept these notions based on so much commentary since the 2016 census details came out.

Was the census question: Do you believe in GOD? Or, are you an atheist? No! People just marked a box for their religion. 30% said they had no religion. Not - no GOD!

From my experience, I would tend to believe that the majority of those 'No Religion' markers legitimately had no religious institutional following of any substance and were being very honest. Once upon a time, these people ticked their nominal religion to believe that this was expected of a decent citizen.

For many, it is not a rejection of GOD, but possibly just a rejection of any institutional religion.

I believe most people worldwide believe in GOD, or least in an all-powerful force or entity. Also, most of the 'No Religion' group as well. For example, Australia is an exceptionally spiritual country, but not necessarily a religious institutional one - with its roots in both the indigenous earthly beliefs and the strong historic Christian beliefs. The constitution and laws of this land are based on Christian principles.

Unfortunately, there is developing a vocal atheistic movement in this country and worldwide. Not content with their own beliefs being personal, they feel it necessary to impose these views on the non-atheists. And in many cases, attack the believers in various ways. They are trying to convert them to atheism. It has happened to me many times since my first book in the *'GOD Today' Series* was published in 2016. They then openly criticise the religious believers if the believers ever dare to espouse their beliefs.

GOD is 'ALIVE' + DIVINE!

GOD is One – Only One!

For Eternity!

GOD Always Was,

Is

and

Will Be

For All Time!

Secularism is Dangerous, Hollow and Leading Humanity to a Catastrophy

Secularism lacks any substantial religious and spiritual depth and belief foundations. It is based on not needing - the spiritual world, the Divine world of GOD, or GOD! It believes humanity is the only strength and power required for a successful world. That all answers lie within the human spirit and entity, not GOD or religion.

How far from the truth could this be!?

For anyone who has experienced or felt GOD in their lives directly or indirectly, this ignoring GOD or preaching against GOD is unfortunate. In all honesty, who hasn't somehow experienced GOD in nature, in goodness (GODness), in prayer or meditation, in other people through what they have said or done, which has had a significant impact on them, etc.? For those why reply, "No experiences of GOD" you really have to wonder what stops them from identifying and acknowledging GOD and GOD's LOVE? These are mostly secular believers. Some of these experiences they have may not show GOD intrinsically. Yet when a person is open to these experiences, GOD will most likely become seen to at least them and maybe others as well. Unless they deliberately turn away from GOD's presence and vigorously deny the existence of GOD, there should be some level of feeling GOD's LOVE and PRESENCE. This is absolutely available for atheists too!

Many people will have direct experiences with GOD, where they know that GOD has just made direct contact in their heart of hearts, e.g. This may happen through any of the experiences listed above. However, GOD does give people direct knowledge of

GOD's presence in various ways, e.g. 'Tears from GOD'. These Tears confirm some message from GOD. When these types of divine Tears flow, GOD's actual presence is often felt.

Secularism is leading humanity to a catastrophe. This needs to be diverted. No room for God? Why not??? When people take on this sort of responsibility without God, human mistakes or ignorance are often exposed. People may come off second best. God is always present to assist in whatever way God desires, sometimes in line with our options and opinions, sometimes not, but come from God's choice. How will we know when the world is deteriorating under secular control?

Firstly the valued, historical, worldly institutions start to crumble. Respect is lost. The individual becomes the centre of the universe. Broad, accepting communities unravel nationalism, communism, narcissism, nihilism, totalitarianism, and many other 'isms', begin to flourish. And eventually, take over more and more as people get lost in the deepening secular world. GOD eventually becomes a distant memory or an unnecessary prop for people to hang on to without divinity. GOD's Love for all people is always available when requested. We can't lose sight of GOD. We NEED GOD more than ever when this secular scenario begins. GOD is waiting for us to call 'Him'. To bring 'Him' into our lives. Once we believe this divine intervention is possible and do this, then the fun, good things start to roll on and into our lives. Secularity begins to get pushed back. GOD starts to come to the fore.

How are we right now relative to the secularism we have just considered? Unfortunately, already our communities are crumbling. Look at the racism, police killings and Afro-American murders in the USA; the growing racism and anti-Church/GOD growth in Australia and Europe. The attempted 'overthrow' of the Capitol building in Washington USA? This is just the start.

211

The lack of respect or even contempt shown to our politicians and the political class. The growing lack of respect for the law and police. The hate-filled reaction to the Church, Islam and other anti-religious/GOD sentiments growing today.

When respect for groups, institutions, religions and individuals within our society dies, our society dies one bit at a time! Until it is all over!!!

But most importantly, when our respect for each other also breaks down, families disintegrate, careers fall, violence and hate increase. Then the world needs to call out to GOD for significant help – through GOD's perfect LOVE for each of us equally!!!

The answer is found in GOD's teachings through the various genuine religions, prayer and religious experiences, etc. GOD is the answer – not the problem!

Listen to GOD's messages, GOD's people and your personal experiences of GOD. And act according to what is for you, the Truth and Love - supported by GOD!

GOD Is The Answer – Not the Problem

When a person is open to these experiences of GOD, GOD will most likely become 'seen' or experienced to at least these aware people and maybe others who are around as well.

Unless they deliberately turn away from GOD's presence and vigorously deny the existence of GOD,

there should be some level of feeling or experiencing

GOD's LOVE and PRESENCE.

Listen and hear God's messages,

God's people and your personal experiences of God.

God is the answer – not the problem!

Media - Relatively Silent on GOD

Much of the western media seems so caught up with various forms of the 'Post-Christian commentary', that it appears to believe, or at least practise, that there is no GOD or at least no need for GOD in their publications! The exceptions are usually from conservative outlets.

Is it a case that most real, open-minded, intellectual and passionate writers and commentators have felt pressured to remain silent? Yet, the Murdoch media is one such supporter of God and religion, religious stories and religious freedoms.

Is this a case of the 'intellectual elite' believing their personal beliefs are real and ignoring the Absolute GOD's reality? You can't change what exists just because you don't believe it. The Truth is the Truth, no matter what. GOD is GOD, no matter what.

One could be forgiven for thinking that the media has finally lost the REAL plot, as all aspects of religion are rarely written or spoken about, except when the anti-church/religious articles appear. Believing that there is no GOD, hence no need for religions, doesn't make God disappear or be irrelevant. God, the creator of everything, is genuine and present in our world. Don't be fooled otherwise by the vocal non-believers.

No matter how cynical the mainstream and social media and population may be, it is our duty from GOD, to tell the Truth for what it is… a massive challenge for a more and more GODless, western world!

Believing in GOD, loving GOD, and responding to GOD's messages, will lead to a more fulfilled, loving and equally-balanced world.

You can't change what exists

just because you don't believe it.

+

The Truth is the Truth, no matter what.

GOD is GOD, no matter what.

No matter how cynical
the mainstream and social
media and population
may be,

it is our duty from GOD,
to tell the Truth for what
it is...

a massive challenge for a
more and more
GODless, western world!

Stop Bullying GOD's People -

Evil by a relative few within the Church

Is it too early to discuss this thesis? I have recently been reflecting on these next three articles, and believe each should now be shared.

The Royal Commission into 'Institutional Responses to Child Sexual Abuse' has last year presented its findings after a five-year term. The horrors of these crimes are still hitting home. The suffering of so many is a constant nightmare. However, the healing process through both law, ethics and commerce is now being dealt with in a systematic, lawful and ethical way. We must let this take its course.

Most young people were well cared for in these schools and institutions. Remember, it was primarily the churches that helped most young people in need of boarding school or institutional care in those days. The state did very little for education (especially the boarding school and institutional care). Hence, statistically, there would obviously be more harm empirically due to the massive difference in the numbers helped by each Church and public/religious institution.

This doesn't make the Church overall bad. Does it show the evil of some within it and the horrible consequences of their actions and the minimal or nil reaction from the Church and others, e.g. police? Yes, it does. Both the management of the perpetrators of such horrific crimes by Church and public and private institutions within and without the Church opens up many Church people and public officials to various levels of guilt. It shows the variation in policing and other community leadership styles over the decades. This era was in a vastly different world with different principles, laws, place of most institutions, roles respected in each decade, etc.

The admission of the horror of paedophilia and child abuse suffered by so many is a justified response. However, it must be proportionate to when it occurred. The great majority of these crimes were committed decades ago. Yes, the Church and other public or private institutions, must answer for their silence and often the support of some key figures within, all that time ago.

It was a small minority of church clergy and religious involved who did affect thousands of innocent children in Australia. Not, the great majority of the clergy or religious! As it is so often unfairly portrayed by the haters!

This Church (Catholic) which bears much of the brunt of these attacks by the haters and non-believers of GOD and the Church, has always been, and still is, an exceptional model of the Love of GOD in action. The small number of the guilty have mostly received their trials and punishments in line with today's law. The small number must be put in the correct context – the considerable majority of the Church members, clergy and lay, are good, loving people who care for many within and without the Church.

The Catholic Church is the second-largest employer in Australia. Only the public servants of the governments are more extensive in number. This helps the Church in so many influential, successful and necessary ways for GOD!

Bryan Foster

References:

Facebook - 1GOD.world:
https://www.facebook.com/groups/389602698051426/

website: https://www.1GOD.world/
Author, books and videos details at http://www.bryan-foster.com/

For a balance of what was said to, and by, the Commission, see Gerard Henderson's: The media, the Commission and the Church speech. The executive director of The Sydney Institute. https://www.catholicweekly.com.au/gerard-henderson-the-media-the-commission-and-the-church/

Stop Bullying GOD's People -

Haters unite against the Church

The other aspect, of bullying GOD's people, needs to be separated and appropriately seen in the light of its reality. The Church is the main target of many - even though many other institutions named by the Commission - many state and non-religious institutions and groups. Why this emphasis? Why the underlying motive?

Anyone who is continually blaming the Church of today for what may have happened decades ago is way off-limits. By all means, criticise and legally charge those involved over the decades. Don't be libellous and hateful though. Don't find people guilty before their trial. Accurate evidence is needed before the trials and within the trials. If those on trial have to appear in court, so should the victims; works for both accused and victim in some format. Without this, how can the evidence be found to be accurate if it goes uncontested in court? It is a fundamental, democratic court principle. The victim's evidence needs to be presented in such a way so as not to cause too much retelling of the story if this is how the court feels.

Hate is not any form of a healer. Don't be disproportionate to today's actual reality, especially knowing how the mainline media and the social media will cover this sort of trial – basically, something along the lines of, 'destroy the Church, GOD's people, and all in it'! But, of course, they will deny it.

What of all the good, wholesome clergy, religious and non-religious lay people who make up today's Church? Many were not even around when these crimes were committed. Most never knew what happened, until recent years. Why try and bring their faith and beliefs down, as well!? Stop trying to kill the Church off, and by this approach stop 'killing' off the most Loving GOD. This is so very evil!! The intellectual elites involved here, show by their arguments, that they have no idea or very little about GOD and GOD's place in all our lives, whether we are directly involved with GOD or not.

Does it make these bullies feel good to try their hardest to bring down GOD's People, the Church? Really!? Because this is what is occurring, whether it is the intention or not. I believe it is often the bullies' deliberate intention.

In any other situation, for any other organisation, this merciless attempt at destruction would be treated with utter contempt by all decent people.

It is also insincere to see the emphasis placed on the Church's response long ago, but nowhere near as much on all the other institutions, which had similar crimes being committed. The secular orphanages, and other state-run and other religions' institutions. Why is it mostly quiet on this front?

To give some perspective, as someone who has taught in Catholic schools for 42 years and attended these schools as a student for a further eight years, I have never seen or heard from anyone at the schools I attended, or at the church where I was an altar boy, of being approached or harmed by any paedophile. Students and staff have spoken on numerous occasions about this possibility, but no-one has experienced this. (My only one experience to the contrary comes from someone who moved interstate and had terrible experiences at his new school interstate.)

For someone who has been involved directly with the Church since my baptism, 60+ years ago, it has become quite apparent that most of these anti-church people come in two main categories. The first is the genuinely, shocked, community members appalled at what happened and how it was treated by those in power, the clergy, and other religions decades ago. The second is the GOD/religion/Church haters.

Nothing highlighted the apparent bias and hate shown by many Catholic church critics, especially crucial media outlets, in the Cardinal Pell court cases. The result of one incorrect guilty finding of the innocent – i.e. Cardinal Pell, was his year-long stretch in jail for the innocent Church leader for something he never did.

How embarrassing for those who may have lied in court or told stories that weren't truthful; maybe due to confusion or possibly false or incorrect support from many others, etc. All the Justices of the Full High Court of Australia unanimously found Australia's Catholic Church leader innocent and had Cardinal Pell released from jail.

All the Justices of the Full High Court of Australia

unanimously found Australia's Catholic Church leader totally innocent

and had Cardinal Pell released from jail.

…as someone who has taught in Catholic schools for 42 years and who attended these schools as a student for a further eight years,

I have never seen or heard from anyone at the schools I attended, or at the church where I was an altar boy, of being approached or harmed by any paedophile.

Students and staff have spoken on numerous occasions about this possibility, but no-one has experienced this in our local Catholic schools.

…most of these anti-Church people come in two main categories.

The first is the genuinely, shocked, members of our Church and community who are appalled at what happened and

how it was treated by those in power, the clergy and other religious.

The second is the GOD/religion/Church haters.

Stop Bullying GOD's People

Haters' alternatives are horrific and evil

The other group and I believe the largest component, are the haters. These people are part of a deliberate move against the Church. Against GOD! Their whole intention is entirely evil. They will not settle until the Church is destroyed and no longer exits, at least with any authority within this world. Until GOD is seen as a falsehood and something only fools would believe in…

Anti-GOD, anti-religion secularists, would be quite happy for an alternative existence without the Church, religion and GOD.

This alternative existence has already been real in many people's lifetime. It still exists. It comes under the title of communism or totalitarianism. No religion, no GOD. During these times, hundreds of millions of people were tortured, falsely imprisoned or killed. You only have to examine Russia's histories, the Soviet Union, China and Cambodia, to name a selection, to gather these atrocities as being quite normal for each country. The numbers killed during these regimes far exceed the numbers killed during all the religious wars combined. Those who lead these holy wars were often blinded by the real expectations of a loving GOD. Secularists fail to acknowledge any of these realities!

Do Australia and the western world want this alternative? Because this is the next force which will fill the void when GOD and religions are destroyed. The principles which are the firm basis of the laws of the western world. The freedom, liberty and justice we all aspire to and have as our founding principles in law are Christian principles, GOD's principles, which have stood the test of time.

Just examine the manifestos of the alternative thinkers, political movements and parties, which seek an end to the Christian principles. Acting mostly innocuously and without any fanfare. They are working beneath the mainstream institutions, so as not to be exposed, ridiculed and stopped!

When someone claims Human Rights, these are the Social Justice Principles of Christianity. Rewriting history or pretending that your ideas are new and should be followed, shows absolute blindness to reality, history and GOD's place within it! Many other examples exist.

GOD is not dead! The Church and other genuine religions are not destroyed but are now needed more than ever! Good people must stand up and not be taken as fools by the insidious, evil ways, beliefs and actions of the minority, hedonistic, secularists and their often-evil agendas, sugar-coated or hidden from view to please, or hide from, the masses – no matter what political movement, party or philosophy they may have linked themselves!!!

This will be quite a challenging era coming up worldwide with social media, the internet and very vocal anti-GOD, anti-Church activists pushing their evil views as the truth. Anything anti-religion is absolutely wrong. There are no such things which are legitimate views against GOD and the Church. Yes, when wrongs are done by members of the Church, government institutions, etc., these must be fixed both ethically and legally. The Church cannot be perfect, being such a massive group of people worldwide, some will at times do wrong. Out of GOD's absolute love of 'His' people, each individual comes with complete freedom to decide their actions. Depending on the severity, legal or other ethical actions will be needed for justice sake.

Fear of being a Religious Person Today?

There seems to be developing a certain amount of fear amongst religious followers and those contemplating following a particular religious faith. There is a fear by many to follow their GOD; such is the venom of the anti-GOD, anti-religious activists!

This fear may also be linked to the latest Australian census data. The misinterpreted '30% for 'No Religion' category was causing quite an amount of unnecessary and unfounded angst in many religious followers and doubters alike. Some interpreted this as a, 'there is no GOD selection'. Others weren't against religion or GOD, just against their selection of having no institutional faith. And a small percentage would have been against having a religion themselves.

Various people within the secular, agnostic and atheistic groups are either deliberately or unknowingly placing negative pressures on those of faith, the believers! There is developing this individualistic view, which is if you are following GOD, then you must be ignorant, fatalistic or just a fool stuck in another millennium or some vortex beyond reality! A view which doesn't allow for personal beliefs or individual differences. In fact, to have these views is considered with contempt by many of these people.

These scaremongers may come from various paradigms of belief ranging from the falsely informed academic or political elite to being caught up with so much of the ill-informed nonsense views that sweep across our social and mainstream media.

So often these days, it becomes almost impossible to know fact from fiction or authentic well-founded and articulated beliefs from personal, individualistic, uninformed ones. It is not just a case of, "This is my personal ('uninformed') belief; therefore, it is correct!" or "Everyone has a right to their opinion!" True, but what if is wrong? If it is wrong, it is wrong, no matter what! But what is wrong here? Many things, especially not believing this Truth from GOD. Also, if it is correct, it is right, no matter what!

In this case, whatever happened to the Aussie dictum of giving everyone a fair go? Of being tolerant and accepting of various thoughts, feelings and beliefs? Values which impress many cultures and faiths worldwide. GOD's dogma, teachings and other faith stances are always correct when coming from GOD. This still allows for discussions, but only to find the Truth which GOD has advanced to all. It is not a case of anything goes! That everyone's opinions are right! Those disbelievers who only believe that their view is correct and don't respect anyone else's GOD views have stifled necessary debate and forced their incorrect, unsubstantiated opinions on to everyone. There is enough evidence stating the Truth of this from various Revelations, inspired messages and discernment from GOD over the years.

The growing political and academic 'elite' of extremists need to be called out for what they are and what they do to our society's generous and accepting fabric. Something many countries can only dream of while suffering the totally INCORRECT NO GOD faith propagated by their leaders. No more ridiculing of differences! No more 'elite' grandstanding! It is becoming quite apparent for many, if not most, within this western democratic, pluralistic culture, that an unknown number of countries are forcing their political views, dressed up as values or ethics of a non-religious country, onto the academic universities, various businesses and selected politicians, being affected nationwide. If happening here, it would be a fair guess that other countries are also suffering similar hacks, known or unknown.

Let's Go – NOW the FACTS.

GOD Exists. This book's premise is a belief in the ONLY ONE GOD and GOD's Love for all, equally. The assumption is that GOD exists absolutely in our world – no matter what the unbelievers state! This belief is not up for discussion. It is the world's #1 Truth forever.

#1 Truth is GOD EXISTS ABSOLUTELY!

#2 Truth is GOD = LOVE!!!

#3 Truth is that GOD Loves every person equally for all time

GOD exists! GOD loves us all equally and without reservation! No matter what some may think!

I am sure most of these activists would be unhappy knowing of the 21 Revelations I received directly from GOD in 2016 and 2018. They would claim that this is impossible because they don't believe it and are ignorant of GOD's Love, GOD's reality, and GOD's Love of them - as much as for any other human ever. The evil people (GOD's Blasphemers, etc.) who outrightly reject GOD and GOD's followers, need to be less ignorant of reality and become searchers of the Truth from GOD.

Love is the Meaning of Life: GOD's Love – is given to all people with no exceptions. Yet, because GOD exists, no matter our thoughts and beliefs, GOD exists – No Questions Asked - *otherwise, you are challenging GOD – we can't challenge GOD on anything!!! No arguments against GOD or GOD's teachings…*

For the deniers and non-believers, it is up to you to genuinely search for GOD, place your trust in GOD to become an active part of your lives, well before your rejection of GOD sets in and steals you away from the search for the Truth, of and from, GOD.

That is if that may become your decision. Being fully informed is absolutely critical for a mature, correct decision (about anything) but particularly about GOD. GOD's Truth is the Truth – no disputes allowed! No challenging of GOD allowed! Questioning of GOD and GOD's teachings, Yes. But disputing GOD, No!

Once honest, authentic people can get a good appreciation of who the activists or the real enemies of GOD and the various religions are, and what their arguments and beliefs are about GOD, then we can all support and encourage our Church/religious leaders and hopefully large groups of the populations to stand up to these uninformed bullies. To call them out for what they are. TO LOVE THEM AS GOD DOES, but to call for no hate, violence, or sometimes vicious attacks verbally, physically or through the written word etc. of the GOD believers.

Their statements and beliefs must come through solid arguments and knowledge of GOD and GOD's teachings through Revelations, scripture and inspired messages, etc. Place the facts and experiences of thousands of years of some mainline religious traditions before them. Once this occurs the fear of following GOD should begin to disappear. GOD's Love will shine through on all of us, good and bad alike.

Taking a fundamentalist approach to the Hebrew scriptures of Judaism (i.e. the Old Testament for Christians) will only confuse most people, due to the apparent violence and retribution etc. contained in many of these scriptures. Scriptural scholars/analysts who interpret these scriptures through the contextualist approach will place the selected sections of scripture into the context of the days and era from which these come. The literal, fundamentalist approach will miss a good deal of detail due to their literal interpretation. Taking scripture word-for-word only allows for a minimal appreciation of GOD's messages for GOD's people today.

With the assistance of GOD through prayer, along with some of the supportive arguments discussed in this article and others throughout the book, people should begin to no longer fear being a follower of GOD and religion. Look after each other. Love each other. You are in the great majority of the world's populations. Pray that our GOD and religious non-believers, the haters, the vicious and the vile, evil rejectors (if this is their deliberate approach) of GOD and religion can start their progress towards understanding and eventually LOVING GOD, various faiths and religious followers.

Have no more fear of being a religious follower. You have GOD and the majority of the world on your side! Call for Godly or people support when in need. LOVE GOD who LOVES you so MUCH that you could never imagine this level of LOVE is at all possible – but it IS and forever?!

Have no more fear of being a religious follower.

You have GOD and the majority of the world on your side!

Call for Godly or people support when in need.

LOVE GOD who LOVES you so MUCH

that you could never imagine this level of LOVE is at all possible –

but it IS and forever?!

Bryan Foster

Heretic

One of the best religious books of the past few years is former Muslim, Ayaan Hirst Ali, 2016, *Heretic: Why Islam Needs A Reformation Now*, Fourth Estate (Harper Collins), N.Y.. It is a watershed presentation of how to understand, appreciate and then act against the aggressive Islamic fundamentalists.

Ali's book on the heresies of her former faith, Islam, explains how the west is misinterpreting what the real purpose of the violence is. According to her lived experience, what the Islamic fundamentalists say is what they mean. It isn't about poverty or disadvantage, as many of these western people claim, even though their financial well-being is seriously challenged, at times.

She believes from her direct experience that they honestly claim that they are defending against those anti-Allah, anti-Islam people being the truth. Many attackers are not poor or disadvantaged she states. They are genuinely in jihad for GOD!

Ali's resume is quite spectacular; it includes: escaping with her family, from her ancestral home in Sudan; her family's escape from Saudi Arabia after seeking refuge there; being a member of the Netherlands parliament, a European parliament, and the recipient of various awards and academic positions at Harvard University, U.S.A..

Exceptionally, unfortunately, because of her publications, presentations and rejection of Islam, she is on a never-ending 'run'. Leaving Islam made her an apostate needing to continually escape from her 'home' to another 'home' regularly.

One would think that her beliefs have made her life unenjoyable.

The highly principled lady, who came from a country in extreme poverty, moved across the world, first escaping to Arab countries with her family, then in Europe gaining a parliamentary seat, and then on to the most extensive and generally considered most powerful and wealthy USA. Here she is protected from the violence chasing her. Her experience, principles and extreme courage are an example for all.

GOD Loves Aayan.

GOD loves you.

GOD Loves you both EQUALLY.

GOD Loves ALL the TIME.

Bryan Foster

Some
Loving
Challenges

Do you Believe in Angels?

ABBA struck a very interesting chord with the song; *I Have a Dream* - to state continually through the lyrics that 'I believe in angels'. Being someone who consistently doubted this reality during my adult years, I changed my appreciation in the last couple of years. I have discerned for me that angels are real. What do you think?

Reasons for this decision were that some coincidental signs which shone through during this period. There was ABBA's song which repeated on me several times during a night of sleep. Another was Greg Sheridan's ('The Australian' newspaper) *GOD is Good for You* book published recently (at time of writing this article). Greg shared his belief in angels, especially in the context of the massive gap between GOD and humanity if there weren't any angels. While a third example is someone I am very close to, whom I believe is an angel, or at least has the characteristics which I believe an angel would have - very spiritual, very loving, wanting the very best for all people, living a wonderful and wholesome life and offering exceptional advice when needed. Do you know any angels? Or angel-like people?

Another unrelated experience seemed to point towards this angel belief. An aura reading while at Crystal Castle in the hinterland outside Byron Bay was something quite special. There was an enveloping light which seemed to point towards something exceptional – could this be my unique angel? I realise much of this may be far beyond reality, but I feel encouraged to share it.

Having such a massive change in belief is quite confronting. Yet, I believe now in the existence of angels - now coming the full circle from my innocent young childhood belief in angels to a strong adult belief today, many decades later.

Do the Devil & Hell Exist?

One of today's favoured topics and the past few decades but very rarely spoken about in public is the devil. There seems this intrinsic belief these days that there is no devil. Some go further and believe in Hell. Others believe that no matter what they do wrong, GOD will automatically forgive them of everything, and they will end up in Heaven – not correct. GOD's total forgiveness, essential for Heaven, is granted to those who are fully and genuinely sorry for their sinfulness and have sort forgiveness from GOD, along with the others who were hurt and leading to the sinners' forgiveness of themselves personally.

Fundamental followers of many religions believe in the devil. Their belief is based on a literal interpretation of their scripture and holy books, i.e. taking the written message word for word as the truth. The more liberal religions and denominations of those mainline religions and others interpret their scripture more from a contextual viewpoint, i.e., what the author/s meant for the day and age when written or orally told. They were then relating this to today.

Based on many decades of inspired messages from GOD, my personal discerned belief is that there is no devil as such, but there is definitely considerable evil throughout this world. Sin occurs when WE choose to do something against GOD or GOD's teachings knowing this to be wrong. When this happens, the person is selecting No GOD to GOD for that moment in time. The person, through their free will, is freely moving away from GOD. Evil influences many of our decisions and choices. It is we who are making a choice. It isn't the devil or GOD or anyone else. We are responsible for our own decisions, nobody else is.

These choices we make, good, bad or indifferent, are our personal choices. We then must take full responsibility for these decisions.

The concept of the 'devil' does exist but in the form of the literal force of evil. Evil people or people's evil influences, etc., impact on us and our decisions. There is no actual gigantic evil forceful pushing us towards an evil outcome. It was relatively easy historically for people to explicitly believe in the devil. Why? Without being flippant, humanity often craves a 'goody' and its counterweight, the 'baddie'. It is readily accepted and understood. Yet, in this circumstance, the reality is way beyond humanity's ability to comprehend. I have discerned that there is no devil. There is so much evil in our world, especially in various peoples' beliefs and behaviours, though, that convince other people to react sinfully or just be sinful from choice.

After our lifetime on earth, there will be one final option for everyone, no matter how evil, to turn back to GOD. This is because GOD is Absolute Love and by definition, gives everyone a final chance - Absolutely. At the moment of a person's death, GOD will give the person one last chance to decide on GOD or no GOD. Those who choose no GOD will be banished to Hell.

Hell is an existence where the evil people exist in total isolation from each other, without ever being a chance to return to GOD. Catholics also believe in an existence called Purgatory, where the person who died chose GOD but wasn't pure enough actually to go straight to Heaven. It is believed by many Catholics, that while in Purgatory, these people continue their growth and movement through their Free Will to GOD in Heaven. Once perfection is reached in Purgatory, GOD welcomes the person to an eternity in Heaven.

...there is no devil as such,

but there is definitely considerable evil throughout this world.

Evil occurs when WE choose to do something against God or God's teachings knowing this to be wrong.

When this occurs, the person is choosing - No God - for that moment in time.

At the moment of a person's death,

God will give each person one last chance to decide on God or no God...

Heaven or Hell.

Those who choose - no God - based on each person's former lifestyles and beliefs, etc. will be

banished to Hell forever.

Following GOD Enriches Humanity's Love – Be Truthful and Not Greedy

Why does so much of humanity believe, think, or in their own eyes 'know', that to follow GOD with any depth is going to 'take the fun and exhilaration out of life'? How could these people be so far from correct? Let's see why.

The common feeling is that being a so-called 'goody goody' gets you nowhere. Your life will be dull and boring - so many others will be having 'fun'! There is a so-called human demand for good people – 'Get a Life'! Especially for those who are genuinely loving, religious and believe in GOD.

Surely people don't think that life is fun when they hurt others, or themselves, through their desire to 'have fun', etc. GOD's way is the ideal of fun, rewarding, challenging, but ultimately REAL; don't be fooled any other way. Being Truthful and not Greedy adds so much to the quality of life and relationships with GOD and people. Being Truthful and not Greedy were the first two of fifteen Revelations from GOD to me in 2016.

Look at any of GOD's messages to us and see if this is so. Let us consider in more detail those couple of the Revelations in *Where's GOD? Revelations Today* (2018).

1. *Be Truthful.* How can this be considered a negative? Isn't telling the truth a primary belief to benefit us all? Why do we intrinsically dislike liars? Who gains when the truth is acted against? Obviously, not good truthful people, but those who choose bad/wrong! Someone is hiding something etc. from other/s. So to be untruthful is pulling yourself down from a good loving relationship with GOD. Why would a good person hide from the truth? It

is to their benefit being truthful unless they have done wrong and hurt or harmed others. The untruthful people are harming themselves. For what? Their greedy selves!

2. *Don't be Greedy.* How can anyone legitimately argue against this? Greed means someone ends up with more than needed, and others have less. When this goes to extraordinary amounts of greed, then many people are doing without. Often, without the necessities for a decent life. Why do certain people aim for this across their lifestyle and existence? Often arguing and/or believing that whatever they can get is right for them! It becomes a matter of how much more I can continually gain for myself, my family and my associates. It is never enough! Too much Greed!

Without any doubt whatsoever, our lives definitely become enriched by living GOD's commandments and teachings. This is primarily through loving others; in whatever form of love, is dependent on the specific relationship. Following GOD can only make our lives more fulfilled, enjoyable and rewarding. With the enormous bonus of heading in the correct direction to Salvation with GOD in Heaven.

Our lives become enriched by living God's commandments and teachings.

Primarily through **loving others**;

in whatever form of love, is dependent on the specific relationship.

Following GOD can only make our lives more fulfilled, enjoyable and rewarding.

With the enormous bonus of heading in the correct direction to Salvation with GOD in Heaven.

Are All Humans, Fauna and Flora Soul-Filled and Pure at Birth and have an Eternal Choice to Make at Death!?

Just as we have a minimal appreciation and understanding of GOD and GOD's ways, GOD can do what GOD wants to; it is GOD's call – we have no power over GOD what-so-ever! Given that all living flora, and creatures, especially humans, have souls (the life ingredient from GOD), how do plants and animals decide at the death of their choices for the afterlife? This is unknown by humanity, yet this doesn't change the reality of it. Yes, we don't understand how this occurs, yet to say it is up to GOD. This has become a strong belief for me over the years, through considerable discernment with GOD considering which forms of life with GOD could live on after its death. That plants can apparently react to human touch with responsive electronic impulses, as shown through a music synthesiser, at Crystal Castle, outside Byron Bay in NSW, Australia. It shows another possible level of communication between the two great groups – plants and people. (**See video *'Music of the Plants Crystal Castle'* on YouTube on the efozz1 channel. See URL below at the end of this article.)

What do you think after seeing the video?

Now it's time to get science involved to help us appreciate what and how this will evolve.

Therefore, I am suggesting at the stage of death that this will be a 'personal' and informed decision made by all lifeforms at whatever level of acceptance of GOD as possible as they can make. Of course, with God's assistance for the decision as needed. Every living being or living fauna will probably be given those choices! No existent, flora or fauna, will be left out for an answer from GOD. The response from GOD will go directly to the living organism. GOD will ask for the people's, flora's or fauna's choice of where they would want to exist after death. If these life forms choose GOD or the opposite of total loneliness in Hell, it will be their 'personal decision' made with GOD!

For those humans, animals or plants that say, 'Yes' to GOD and all GOD's divine ways, there will be life with GOD and all those heavenly spirits in perfect harmony with GOD in Heaven. Just as people are given that final, absolute choice to be with or without God at that moment of death for eternity, it is believed so by this author, for all the other living creations of God - fauna or flora. Time and discernment will tell if this last belief is real.

Through considerable life encounters, it has been found that when we experience God in the living nature 'He' created, we can feel so at peace, so contented and feel the incredible amount of Love emanating from all the living creations of God. *Personally, I very much enjoy sitting outside amongst the natural flora before going to sleep at night. This similar feeling also occurs in the morning, this time with the awakening birds of so many species.*

These experiences are highly recommended. I firmly believe that you can't rush in forcefully and then discover nothing due to this haste. All these growth stages with God take time. Sit and allow the growth to occur over time. It should eventually envelop you, wrapping you awesomely in the love of God. Stay open and stay aware of this possibility.

The intrinsic call to love nature is often very powerful for many, if not most, people. When we can share these happenings with our loved ones, our Love of them also increases – this is God sharing absolute love with one another, through nature's LOVE from GOD.

Some of these experiences and beliefs come from **Crystal Castle's flora show. You may be quite challenged but hopefully, find this both informative and exciting.

GOD will ask for the people's, flora's and fauna's choice at death of where they would want to exist after death. If these life forms choose GOD or the opposite of total loneliness in Hell, it will be their unique decision made with GOD! For those humans, animals and plants that 'say', 'Yes', to GOD in GOD's divine ways, unknown to us humans at this stage, there will be eternal life with GOD and all those heavenly souls/spirits in perfect harmony with GOD in Heaven. How the plants and animals relate and communicate with GOD is still a mystery. Yet, I firmly believe that these communications eventuate whenever a living plant or animal dies.

For the doubters of this belief, just look into the eyes of any pets you may have. For most pets, there is definitely emotion, including some form of love there! What is the draw to rainforests, coral reefs, deserts, oceans, lakes, gardens, trees and all the plants, etc.? If you laugh at tree huggers due to their somewhat strange relation with trees, maybe think again? Try it yourself! For some reason, just being with these various types of flora brings a deep attachment with us.

A certain deep peacefulness may be present for many people? A calming tranquillity washes over us. There is undoubtedly an experience of GOD being present! Sharing a genuine Love between each party: divine, human and plant!

GOD + People + Animals and other living Creatures + Plants and Trees…

This is our universe with GOD beyond the Earth.

Yet – our end of life options began through our earthly lives. We can all be ONE in Heaven if this is our choice at death. Each living entity chooses Heaven or Hell, after death, with GOD. This unique choice is dependent on the sort of lifestyle led by each on Earth, i.e. by the place, we each chose for GOD throughout our lives, through our ethics and beliefs, etc.

** Crystal Castle, west of Byron Bay, NSW, Australia – by the author.

> For those humans, animals and plants that
> 'say', 'Yes', to GOD in GOD's divine ways,
> which are unknown to us humans at this stage,
> there will be eternal life with GOD
> and all those now heavenly souls/spirits
> in perfect harmony with GOD in Heaven.
> How the plants and animals relate and
> communicate with GOD
> is still a mystery?

https://www.youtube.com/watch?v=7U_z0MUo4MQ
(* 'Mahomad' was spelt this way by GOD when revealing the first of the 21 Revelations to me in 2016.)

How would we react if Jesus, Mahomad, Moses
or Brahman walked into the room? ...

I have a funny inkling, even in this world of so
much of everything, yet so little of God, that
people would initially freeze! Wonder? Question?
Even challenge!

Then most would rush over to do it [a selfie]!...

RELIGIOUS LOVE SOLUTIONS

Introduction to Religious Solutions

There can only be one genuine response for this section's title - GOD.

What GOD offers us all as a solution is Absolute LOVE from 'HIM'.

With this LOVE comes the extraordinary reality of GOD's FORGIVENESS. No matter what we do. No matter how evil our sinfulness. If we are authentically sorry and seek forgiveness from God and those affected, and hopefully also offer restitution to the one/s hurt, including ourselves, GOD will forgive us. Heaven then awaits us when we die.

The FREE WILL we have all been freely given from our ABSOLUTELY LOVING GOD is to decide to be with or against GOD. This is an extra special gift from GOD to choose - YES for GOD; or no for God - and hence be against GOD. Each leads to our physical, life-ending and 'going' to – Heaven (GOD and Perfection) or Hell (Evil and Isolated Rejection) – both forever awaits.

The closer we grow towards GOD and live a LOVING life surrounded by GOD, the greater our sense of TRUE GODLY LOVE for everyone. GOD may send us signs, as an example: coincidences, feelings of loving support and for some, Tears from GOD (See the following article for details on 'Tears from GOD') along with other signs, e.g. Sun and cloud arrows, rays, flares a giant sun cross, etc. Similar to the above ones, various signs become a reality for those getting closer to GOD.

We then consider what other forms of LOVE with which GOD may assist us. Angels, Heaven, hell and evil, which are rarely discussed through our earthly media and social media, are examined here to appreciate how each of these is placed in the cosmos of existence. As well as how this GODLY LOVE may assist us? How we reject evil and all of its attractions is another personal challenge we all will experience over our lifetimes.

Are All Humans, Fauna and Flora Soul-Filled and Pure at Birth and have an Eternal Choice to Make at Death!?

I certainly believe so through discernment and inspiring messages, which has occurred throughout my life from GOD. To be enveloped, cradled and supported by GOD through people, animals and vegetation are personally memorable and extra special - And True. I personally find that just before going to bed at night, I go outside in my back yard and see and especially sense the plants and whatever is in the soon to be darkness surround me. It feels incredibly comforting and Loving. GOD certainly feels present through the flora and small fauna of the night! And then continues well into the morning and day!

Bryan Foster

GOD's Special Loving Gifts for Us

Tears from GOD

My 'Road to Emmaus' experience, my epiphany, the Commitment to GOD Day on my 25th birthday, highlighted something extraordinary from GOD. (See Appendix 1)

It became obvious to me, that when GOD wanted me to know something exceptional was coming from GOD, there would be a passing on of the Tears from GOD. These are not GOD's tears physically, but these are tears from GOD spiritually, which I and others in similar circumstances experience physically, emotionally and spiritually. These are an uncontrollable flow of tears from GOD, not sobbing tears of normal crying tears. You certainly know of GOD's presence when experiencing these.

There is an overwhelming sense of GOD's love and presence being intimately experienced at that moment. Words cannot describe what is happening, as it is very obvious to the recipient that it is on another level beyond the physical. Tears pour out in free flow. There are no typical contorted facial expressions as is typically associated with crying. It isn't crying as we know it, but tears are flowing uncontrollably.

Many others also experience these Tears from GOD. No one religion can claim this existence solely, as it occurs across several religions. This section mainly looks at the place of the tears in Christianity, Islam and Hinduism.

Just as these tears overwhelmed me all those years ago on my 25th birthday at a school's Commitment to God Day, each time GOD needs me to realise that something extra special is happening, or that differentiation is required between things of this world and things GOD wants me to know about or do, or that I need strong support as part of GOD's plan, GOD shares the tears.

Many will say that this is all just emotion and that the tears come because I am emotional about something. Early on, this was my thought too. However, over time, there has developed an evident appreciation of the difference between normal emotional tears and those from GOD.

The difference is very hard to explain, other than to say that the recipient gets this inherent feeling simultaneously as the tears that GOD is making it known that GOD is mostly present at that moment. It is not just like *feeling* GOD's presence but *knowing* GOD is present.

Sometimes you almost hear GOD words, but you know these are your words being inspired by GOD. (See Appendix 3) Many people would appreciate this from their own prayer life when messages come to them from GOD. It is GOD's inspiration but through your thoughtful words.

These Tears from GOD were called on several times, as I went through the development of these *'GOD Today' Series* books. I needed to be continually reminded that the Revelations and inspired messages of the books were correct. In *1GOD.world: One GOD for All* (2016) it was especially needed for the central premise and Revelation being unconditionally accepted before it was published: that there is only one GOD for all religions, peoples and cultures - forever. As well, all the inspired messages within the book up until the Mt Warning Revelation experience had been discerned as correct over several decades, yet reassurance through the Tears from GOD was still needed before publication. Similar support and verification from GOD are necessary for this next book; *Love is the Meaning of Life: GOD's Love.*

With the initial planning done in May 2016 for the first book, it was time to get GOD's approval. I stood with my wife, Karen, in our kitchen one evening and let her know I wasn't sure if the central premise for publication being singled out and emphasised, as I hadn't had any confirmation message from GOD. I was concerned that I might have been overstepping the mark but didn't know-how. At that moment, a rush of tears filled my eyes – Tears from GOD answered my call! The message from GOD was palpable - that it was correct and to go ahead, write the book and publish.

Since that time, there have been various other occasions when this assurance has been given, especially at Mt Warning. One particular example evolved into a video of this topic being recorded with Mt Warning as a background. **

I realise many people will challenge my belief in this. However, all I can say is that I inherently know it is correct and that I have GOD's support and encouragement to state this publicly and forcefully. (See Appendices 3 and 4)

Let us consider where the Tears from GOD historically come from when viewed in the three example traditions of Christianity, Islam and Hinduism.

Christianity has long believed in this phenomenon, often referred to as the 'gift of tears' from the Holy Spirit (GOD). The Holy Spirit freely gives the charismatic gifts. Ewing beautifully encapsulates the closeness with GOD caused by these tears when she highlights how the Holy Spirit is infused into the receiver's soul. The tears' action is the physical sign and personal experience of this bringing about such a result. The person will often be unable to explain what is or has happened - that the experience is somewhat subconscious and in a different realm.

Fenelon states how Pope Francis refers to these as 'the gift of tears'. He emphasises how this helps prepare the receiver to see

Jesus (GOD), and how the concept is based on the 'Spiritual Exercises' of St Ignatius, especially where Ignatius is overwhelmed by the consolation of GOD. The tears are coming from a sense of deep intimacy with GOD, primarily while Ignatius celebrated the Eucharist in all its beauty and presence of GOD's love. She goes on to share theologian Tim Muldoon's thoughts on how the pope sees this as a mystical experience of a deep, preconscious conviction of GOD's presence. It results from an overwhelming experience of receiving GOD's intimate love which can only be expressed through the free-flowing tears.

Fr Bartunek, an evangelical Christian and now a Catholic priest, explain that this gift can occur singularly or on multiple occasions. He states that it doesn't mean the receiver is any holier or closer to GOD than others. He says it is an event to encourage those receiving or witness it to more significant and more substantial relationships with GOD, provide great comfort from GOD, or confirm decisions they had previously made and defend against temptation. Physiologically he notes how these Tears from GOD are not like normal tears, resulting in sobbing due to everyday life's emotions. Still, these tears flow abundantly and freely without any physical tension or facial contortions. He also mentions that this gift isn't in scripture or the Catechism but has been referred to by various spiritual writers ever since the early church.

In 'Al-Islam', examples of tears from GOD are seen in both the Qur'an and traditions. Some examples in the Qur'an include when tears occur as a sign of perceiving the realities of GOD or as a sign of wisdom. Prophets shed tears for Allah when hearing of communications from GOD. Tears are seen as so significant in Islamic tradition that they are a gift to humanity, illuminate and soften the heart and bring about a great reward from GOD, including extinguishing GOD's wrath.

Rattner speaks of what he calls the emotion of devotion, a crying for GOD, which he explores from Hindu and Christian traditions. Similar to both the Christian and Islamic examples above, the tears come from GOD at those special and often unique transformational moments with GOD. These were regular and spontaneous, purifying him to experience higher consciousness states, leading to continual spiritual development.

** See 'Tears from GOD...' video by Bryan Foster at https://www.youtube.com/watch?v=z5mmNvIKko4

Edited Extracts from: *Where's GOD? Revelations Today*, Bryan Foster, 2018, Great Developments Publishers, Gold Coast, p46-50.

'Tears from God'

There is an overwhelming sense of God's love
and presence being intimately experienced at that
moment.

… it is very obvious to the recipient that it is on
another level beyond the physical.

Tears pour out in free flow.

…It isn't crying as we know it,

but tears sent from GOD are flowing
uncontrollably.

'Tears from GOD' – a Truly Loving Example

Per 5 Friday - The last Lesson for Me - EVER - Before Retirement

What a way to retire!

My last full-time class from 42 years blew me away in so many ways! This lesson was a full 45 minutes experience of 'Tears from GOD' for quite a few people. GOD was truly present in the room.

The initial plan to pray, speak about subject choices and a couple of financial saving tips before having free classroom time, didn't get beyond the prayer...

Just after praying the intentions offered for the day, I was about to ask everyone to say our last 'Our Father' prayer together as a group – and then silence. As my tears started to flow, I couldn't begin the prayer aloud. Head bowed, I tried so hard. The students remained absolutely quiet and still. No matter how hard I tried, I couldn't say anything!

Then I looked up and saw one student, looking straight at me, her eyes welled with tears, and there was a mystical sense that everyone knew who was truly in the room with us! A young male student then initiated the Our Father's leadership, and all the students said a most remarkable rendition, with me remaining silent.

As it was completed, one of the students quietly said, "Tears from GOD."

The remainder of the lesson was one of the students wanting to know so much more about the place of the 'Tears from GOD' in

255

my life, and in my recent book writing, and what the next book would be about and how it would eventuate with the help of GOD.

I have never had a group of 15-year-olds in year ten as one with a religious discussion. So empathetic and real. So wanting to share their thoughts and know more. So supportive of their teacher's situation.

Just to be sure I wasn't going too far, I asked them to be brutally truthful and let me know whether they believed me and that I was truthful – to use their inherent 15 years-old 'rubbish-detector' intuition. Unanimous, authentic, strong support followed.

As the discussion came to a natural close after 45 minutes, the bell rang (as if on cue). Sincere thanks and final farewells followed. In a moment of tears from GOD before leaving, one young lady explained how she understood exactly where I was coming from and what was happening to both of us at that moment.

I thanked her sincerely and let her know that there couldn't have been a better, more complete ending to my full-time teaching career.

A couple of interesting points discussed. A young man near the end of the class asked, "What is the highlight of your time at Aquinas?" He almost blew me away, as I had the astonishing realisation that I was living it at that very moment. Couldn't think of another on this scale! So happily said so. He also suggested that the next book is released on the 40th day of next year. We had just been discussing the significance of the number 40 in scripture, especially Moses' 40 years in the desert and Jesus 40 days in the desert. This linked with how my life this year and next has two major 40th events, i.e., 40 years of teaching this year and 40 years of marriage next year.

Free Will

If we assume that the concept of an Absolutely loving GOD exists, it follows that GOD would create the Free Will needed to express human love for and with GOD and the creative world. *This absolute Free Will, in turn, allows all of humanity to make decisions for or against GOD absolutely freely.* We decide individually, and collectively through our various systems and communities, how this world operates, who gains and loses, who and what is valued, and the future direction of people, cultures, countries, etc.

Our societies decide who will get fed, who will live in relative peace, who will be educated and looked after through quality health and welfare schemes.

Individuals and societies also decide who won't!!!

This may seem insensitive, but it is often subconsciously decided or supported by the populous. Or maybe it is, in fact, beyond their understanding or appreciation of how they see their world. Many either consciously or subconsciously ignore the evil or challenges that occur around them within their world.

It is also consciously decided by lawmakers and bureaucrats through how the laws are written and implemented. A just society creates laws and legal processes, which enhance everyone's quality of life, opportunities in life and well-being, etc. Not just the select few, especially those with wealth and political clout. (No entitlement here, GOD says that we are all equal to each other.) Nationalism is also at the core of many decisions. Governments justify their laws regarding protecting their people's best interests (Note that this doesn't usually include people from other countries; unless it is strategically necessary.)

The United Nations has a vital role to play in fighting for a just world. A world where its leaders communicate and devise plans that will enhance all peoples - a world where peace, freedom, and prosperity is the key aim.

Religions and their leaders are called upon by GOD to illuminate a darkened world to see the true Light. To appreciate the power everyone has through their GOD-given Free Will. To encourage all people no matter their religion, culture or nationality to use their, often unknown, enormous clout to save the weak and disadvantaged within their societies and the world. A strong, peaceful, united world based on GOD's #1 principle of LOVE is an outcome too good to be squandered on any level of political or individual greed.

Belief in a loving GOD is exceptionally troubling to many people, as this places the considerable onus on each person. People need to take responsibility for their personal and communal actions, as everything impacts themselves and/or others. Free Will dictates this. *Today, too many people cop out and blame GOD for anything and everything wrong in this world instead of taking that responsibility for their actions.*

GOD desires only good for people and never deliberately harms them. This is not to say that GOD doesn't react or act as we might imagine. GOD has GOD's ways and options for each of us. This leads to us having to make various decisions that impact our lives and others' lives. His life direction for us will at times be what we would like, while at other times GOD's choice may take us into uncharted ways. Many of these will require us using our Free Will in the decision making. GOD also challenges people, often in unexpected ways. These challenges can be from very minor to extremely major and life-threatening.

Once GOD gave us absolute freedom to decide out of Absolute Love for us, then the evil, badness, and downright harm people deliberately do to others result from their Free Will. GOD can't be evil because GOD is the opposite of evil; these people are evil, and GOD is Love. Because of absolute freedom,

GOD allows things to run their natural course. It is up to us to take the leadership needed for developing the best Loving, peaceful, compassionate world we desire.

Unfortunately, most things which hurt people, have been done by humans and their free choices. Wars, violence, abuse, non-sharing of the worldly wealth causing poverty, various options related from human lifestyle choices, e.g. resulting from poorly chosen diets, smoking, alcohol and various illegal drugs, etc., lack of fitness and everyday well-being, unsafe places and circumstances in which people choose to live, etc. A number of these has to do with a lack of information, education and life opportunities, especially for the poor and otherwise disadvantaged. These people are much more likely to be harmed by other people's decisions than the well off, and educated people may be.

We must be aware that there is also a dimension of mystery from GOD in all of this? Meaning basically – there is GOD's 'stuff' about what we don't know much. Stuff we don't know how to handle or wonder what to do with it, or even why it's here, etc.

Because GOD is not of our physical world and is not physical but is divine and GODly, we cannot imagine with any real certainty, why GOD allowed for some natural events to occur? Sometimes ending with people getting harmed or hurt in various ways. There is some clue, though, when we accept that many people claim to have gained from some form of suffering or loss; and that their lives have been challenged and even enhanced, etc. Another aspect of life – including - life, suffering, joy, death

Suffering is also an opportunity for people to grow closer to GOD. It could be considered as GOD calling to the affected people to engage with GOD. We NEED GOD, intrinsically. Don't try and hide from GOD but be 'loud and proud', in your natural way.

Bryan Foster

We know that out of GOD's Absolute Love and our own Free Will, GOD, has to allow people to make bad choices with the various ramifications resulting. The answer as to why awaits us through our salvation with GOD in Heaven. We don't know when GOD will be calling us at death. Another mystery.

The One GOD of the universe, loves all of creation so much, that no harm is desired on any person. Humanity is the pinnacle of living creations. Society has Free Will and the capacity to create or destroy our world.

> Many people know that out of GOD's Absolute Love and our own Free Will,
>
> GOD, has to allow people to make bad choices with the various ramifications resulting.
>
> The answer as to why awaits us through our salvation with GOD in Heaven.
>
> We don't know when GOD will be calling us at death. Another mystery.

The One GOD of the universe,

loves all of creation so much, that no harm is desired on any person.

Humanity is the pinnacle of living creations.

Society has Free Will and the capacity to create or destroy our world.

It's up to all of us!!!

(Edited Extract from *Where's GOD? Revelations Today*, Bryan Foster, 2018, Great Developments Publishers, Gold Coast, p. 51-53)

Perfection vs Non-perfection

Only one entity in the universe is perfect, and that is the GOD of the world, which has always existed and will exist for eternity for all people, forever. When we are told that we are made in the likeness of GOD, that is referring to all those unique human qualities which GOD has given us. These include the ability to love, forgive, have compassion, etc., to build good friendships and relationships, be communal and work for each others' well-being, etc. We don't look like GOD, as we are physical, and GOD is the divine/spirit/entity.

But most importantly, to be able to pray to GOD and build this relationship so that it can be as good as we can make it.

GOD made each of the billions of people who have been on this earth, are on this earth, or will be on this earth. Each is unique and equally as special to GOD. GOD has no favourites. He made them as 'perfect' as He desired. No-one is perfect, though, as we all have the Free Will to choose against GOD, i.e. to sin! And we all do it, at least sometimes. No-one is perfect in any way. Many are close. Even more, try to be. However, as our western world is so very well off compared to the other second and third worlds, our relationship with GOD is far less than should be and could be. We are often the result of everything our world offers, at least for most of us. We seem to lose the need for GOD! How incredibly selfish is this?

Who do most people call to when they are in trouble or having serious difficulties, etc.? GOD!

As soon as people can acknowledge the perfection of GOD and GOD's place in everything, we, the imperfect, will begin the quality journey to GOD. This should always be our primary aim – to search for and find GOD!

We only have to 'impress' GOD, not our fellow humanity. We impress GOD by firstly acknowledging his superiority and leadership over us and then following GOD's commandments, teachings and lifestyle. GOD's 'rules and regulations' exist for the betterment of us all. When we follow GOD correctly, great things happen. We even gain a better appreciation of what is truly important in our lives and knowing what to do. For example, our physical traits don't require repair, because GOD gave each of us what we need appearance-wise in all ways.

Being an imperfect human person is actually the gift from GOD we are. Everyone has imperfections, no matter how hard we try to remove these, and some can be quite successful with this. We are still the imperfect aiming for legitimate, authentic perfection, as can realistically be attained with all our imperfections and faults.

As a population, we certainly waste enormous amounts of money trying to look a certain way, be a specific type of person, have a particular image to maintain, gain various 'bonus points' from those we try to impress, etc. And all for what?

As a population, we certainly waste enormous amounts of money trying to look a certain way, be a certain type of person, have a certain image to maintain, gain various 'bonus points' from those we try to impress, etc.

And all for what?

Forgiveness

Forgiveness is a most challenging process but an essential need within all humans. Forgiveness is a central tenant of love. Love of GOD and others. In our human relationships, forgiveness is vital.

People need to forgive others for their wrongdoing towards them. Others need to forgive us for our failings. We need to forgive ourselves. Forgiveness offered and received is essential for the relationship to repair and grow.

Of course, this is not a simple procedure or one with an inevitable outcome. It depends on so much. It depends on our openness to forgive and to be forgiven. It depends on the person we hurt, who hurt us, being open to forgive, or accepting forgiveness. It sometimes depends on our ability to offer restitution knowingly or unknowingly to the recipient. It depends on our experience of forgiveness and how we have been affected previously. It depends on our personality, mental, physical and social health, on our standing with the person concerned, and on so much more.

Once we can forgive and be forgiven and affect restitution, if necessary, we are set free. We can live more peaceful, fulfilling lives. Our relationships are healthier, and we are happier within these. We are more complete as people living in our families, workplaces, communities, etc.

We must also appreciate and accept GOD into our earthly relationships. We need to invite GOD into our relationships, to help strengthen these and be there when difficulties arise. When this happens, GOD supports us and helps us work through the challenges, until the final loving outcome is achieved.

Primarily, out of love, we are required to place GOD as the number one in our lives and our relationships. When we can accept this, and turn our relationships over to GOD, we are then open to receive so much assistance willingly and accept the outcomes, as part of GOD's plan.

This is very freeing and something we need to work towards.

Apologising to GOD for our hurt caused and the wrongdoings done, adds another dimension to our improvement and relationship with GOD. GOD always wants the best for, and of, each of us. GOD knows intrinsically that we will weaken and make mistakes, hurting ourselves and others along the way. We can't hurt GOD, but we can freely move away from GOD through our thoughts and actions. Our acknowledgement of these wrongs and hurts helps the healing process and brings us back closer to our GOD relationship. This is GOD's desire for us.

GOD loves each of us so much that GOD needs us all to be as close as possible to each other and GOD - in true love.

(Edited Extract from *Where's GOD? Revelations Today*, Bryan Foster, 2018, Great Developments Publishers, Gold Coast, p. 179-180)

Forgiveness is GODliness

What is forgiveness? Forgiveness is an essential and critical aspect of love. Without forgiveness, we can't realign ourselves with the good in ourselves and others. Linguistically another term for goodness - goodliness can be - GODliness!

i.e. GOD=Absolute Good = Absolute LOVE

When we freely and genuinely seek forgiveness from GOD, others and ourselves, we are cancelling out the bad and freely recreating the good we have inside - in our true selves.

As humans, our natural desire is for happiness, enjoyment, freedom, success, compassion, empathy, etc. - all critical aspects of genuine love.

When we are hurt emotionally, socially or physically, etc., we may lose sight of our loving relationships for that moment in time. A low point from which we then need to strive forward to get back on the 'good' track of life. Forgiveness is now essential for this.

We need to forgive others for hurting us. We need others to forgive us for the harm we caused them. We need to forgive ourselves to 'clean our slate' - to remove the nastiness or hate etc. we have caused ourselves or others.

Once we have forgiven these various people, including ourselves, we move back closer to each of those concerned. We also move back to GOD after seeking forgiveness and purity, which is ours genuinely claimed. Once all our sins have been forgiven, we then exist in a state of purity (until next, we sin).

Purity should be our aim and desire throughout life. Our virtue helps inspire and bring others to be likewise – pure!

God NEEDS us all to be as close as possible

to God

and each other

- in true love.

God loves each of us so much… Absolutely.

Forgiveness

is essential for a

Loving Life.

LOVE NEEDS FORGIVENESS

FORGIVENESS BRINGS LOVE!

Beautiful Example of Forgiveness

There are so many beautiful examples of forgiveness, which challenge humanity to do the right thing and forgive others and ourselves. This is dependent on the circumstances but is essential to our healing and that of others.

An excellent example of forgiveness essential for healing is shown by the beautiful Muslim father who forgave his little son's accidental killer. An absolute inspiration for humanity!

Mr Darwich, father of Jihad, one of the boys killed in the school car crash in Melbourne, Australia, in 2017, offered the ultimate forgiveness to the driver of the car which killed his son in this horrible accident.

One of the most challenging aspects of life is forgiving those who have harmed us, especially when harmed beyond imagination.

This is truly a divine act by a loving human being - an absolute lover, believer, and GOD follower.

His Islamic faith is giving him incredible strength.

...the beautiful Muslim father who forgave his little son's accidental killer.

An absolute inspiration for humanity!

...His Islamic faith is giving him incredible strength.

Who's strongly supporting GOD in today's world? – Islam & Christianity?

The biggest supporters include those whom we may disagree with vehemently. Yet, in their minds, they are fighting for GOD out of Love for GOD. While what seems like a large percentage of the western world, ignores the necessity to follow GOD or any religion! How many positive news articles have been about GOD in our major Western media companies in the past few years? The Love for GOD and each other is essential for deeply loving others in our lives. Love breeds Love.

Australia is a secular country in general, and probably at the forefront of 'seeming not to need GOD' and in many cases actively 'fighting' against GOD. Two examples highlight this: when was the last time you heard anyone in the ALP or Greens political parties in Australia, publically say that their prayers and thoughts were with those who were suffering some tragedy? Yes, their 'thoughts' were, but no mention of a need for GOD's assistance, as far as I could ascertain.

It seems this, for example, is more common in Australia than in the USA? The 'GOD of Christianity' appears to play a much larger part in the USA publically. What about the wealthy offering to fully or mostly share their wealth with the poor for a genuinely egalitarian, fair and loving nation as commanded by GOD? Incidentally, Australia is probably the most egalitarian country worldwide. There seems to be a high level of spirituality and belief in GOD in general, just not any serious following of a specific religion publically, overall.

Yet, Australia seems to be very supportive of Christianity when needed. The country's laws are based on Christian principles.

Some time back at mass at Bangalow, northern NSW, Australia, as the priest mentioned the epiphany of the three 'wise' men in the Christmas nativity story, I found myself wondering who was really putting GOD first in their proclamations and beliefs - reacting to their personal and communal epiphanies. Who was getting out there and using the media, social media, public gatherings, political movements, churches, etc., for GOD's proper place in our world?

Was it the Christians, e.g., as portrayed through the nativity symbols? Gold for worldly leadership, frankincense for religious leadership and myrrh for death. Three characteristics, as shown through the life of Jesus, fully GOD and fully Man. Jesus = Incarnation of GOD.

What religion in today's world places GOD, religion, relationships and communities as their top beliefs and values? Who are prepared to risk all this in the name of GOD? *Islam appears to be the answer. The followers' differences are mainly around the place of violence, particularly the Islamic Shia and Sunni denominations and their Medina and Meccan histories and differences in their understandings of the use of violence.* We can never agree to the innocent murder of civilians or illegal military deaths. We can not agree with the death penalty from any religion. Terrorism is never to be accepted. Violence is anathema to GOD out of Love for all. (See 'Heretic' book by Ayaan Ali. Details in the bibliography.)

Allah/GOD is strongly supported and strongly defended in Islam. Muslims very much place GOD as Number One, in whatever society they live. Unfortunately, many people misunderstand the Qur'an and put too much emphasis on their interpretation of Sharia law. Islamic law and Christian law have many similarities – especially concerning peace and Love of each other and of GOD. Any teaching supporting violence or the death penalty is impossible for a Loving GOD! The Muslim leaders worldwide need to explain their beliefs concerning being against violence and then teach all their followers against it. This contrasts with what is happening in many western communities, particularly Australia, where non-Muslims often call this out as being non-Australian behaviour and beliefs. Many Australians and the numbers are growing, don't see the need for heavily supporting and being directly involved with GOD or religion publically – most likely because they have so much goodness from life and life's opportunities, careers, income, education and leisure time etc. and don't see any relevance or NEED for GOD! In their eyes, what more could they want? This seems selfish to the fairminded.

Peace-loving Muslims, (the great majority of the world's Muslims) who are against violence, have much to teach us, all religions and cultures about GOD and communicating with GOD and centring their lives around GOD. GOD/Allah is the ONE! There is only ONE GOD, the same GOD, for all religions. (See Book 1 in this *'GOD Today' Series - 1God.world: One God for All.*) All genuine religions worldwide can learn so much from Islam and the place of GOD in their daily lives. Their place of prayer, said five times per day, in itself is something compelling when observed from the outside.

It is much more than just being peace-loving, it means placing GOD as Number One and allowing all our beliefs and values to permeate from GOD's teachings. GOD is the answer!

Islam and Christianity both strongly support their religions and GOD/Allah when needed, and in the way, they do this. Islam is far more public, though, especially those from Islamic countries. Christians are generally quieter, yet still very supportive in their ways and beliefs of GOD.

Due to [Aayan Ali's] unquestionably lived experiences on both sides of the Reformation and Islamic argument,

she will help Islam considerably to achieve its desired peaceful outcomes.

It is much more than just being peace-loving,

it means placing GOD as Number One and

allowing all our beliefs and values to permeate

from GOD's teachings. GOD is the answer!

Islam and Christianity both strongly support their religions and GOD/Allah when needed,

and in the way, they do this.

Islam is far more public, though, especially those from Islamic countries.

Christians are generally quieter, yet still very supportive in their ways and beliefs of GOD.

Two Reformations Needed – Secular and Islamic

Genuine Love seems to be deteriorating across the world. So much to do with politics, greed, selfish people, and so on, only looking after themselves. Many will claim it's the way the world is now. Why? The world is still no worse off than it has even been; our problems and challenges are just different but still impact us in various ways. Where is GOD in this? Genuine Love needs to be rediscovered. The place of GOD in Loving relationships needs to take a much more significant role in today's world.

The world needs two new Reformations. Both the Western and Islamic worlds urgently need reform. But for the opposite reasons. One to be more religious (Secular world), the other to enter the 'new' world (Islamic world). A better balance is needed.

The Western secular world needs to re-find those beliefs and principles from which their whole society is based and developed. To then move away from a secular, hedonistic, selfish, greedy society and find GOD again.

The Muslim world needs to have a Reformation searching for the enlightened outcomes that eventuated from the original Reformation and Renaissance periods of the 14th to 17th centuries. Islam needs to be challenged by such activists and dissidents, such as Ayaan Hirst Ali, a fellow at Harvard University's John F. Kennedy School of Government. Ali notes five areas needing specific reform: Mahomad's status and the literalist reading of the Qur'an; life before death; Islamic law and its enforcement and the imperative to wage jihad (p27).

GOD and religion are a necessity and need to be an integral part of our world. Otherwise, our lack of direction from GOD will see the world end as we know it.

Muslims and Christians both strongly support their religions and GOD/Allah when needed,

and in the way, they do this.

Islam is far more public, though, especially for those from Islamic countries.

Christians are generally quieter, yet are still very supportive in their ways and beliefs of GOD.

Secular Reformation Needed Now

A massive change in direction for the Western world and its populations' attitude is needed very quickly. The world, as we know, it is dying.

Our civilisation is now destroying itself. It is wasting our earthly resources like nothing before. It is destroying people and communities like never before. It is very much on its way out! No longer are other individuals and communities fully valued or even respected. The 'Me' world rules. The 'whatever I believe and think is correct' dominates. 'I am but an island, and there is nothing else of importance – anywhere' - echoes from pillar to screen.

There appears to be little place for higher-order values. A small place for genuinely unique, loving, forgiving people. A little place for GOD. This is a guaranteed recipe for disaster.

The onus of contemporary proof of everything has taken the world to the brink.

That everything must be proved by Science is outrightly rejected.

Science can only prove or disprove within the physical world. Science doesn't prove or disprove that higher forces exist.

Science can't prove or disprove GOD.

We need to call out those intellectual elites, atheists and secular fundamentalists who see nothing but the here and now as being real. That nothing is everlasting.

Freedom of speech is dying. The overly politically correct subjugate what it is to be truly human - with all humanity's warts and all, including their various opinions on any topic of interest.

Idealism should be aimed for, but realistically. Following the various religious scriptures with a contextualist approach will help guide us. A literalistic interpretation (taking the teachings literally) of these scriptural sources often leads to misunderstandings and even more problems.

Domestic violence in any of its forms in any level of society is never acceptable. Yet, this form of violence is tearing families and relationships apart in all sections of society. We must all stop this in whatever way we can, individually or communally.

The right to stand up for our real, loving GOD is being destroyed by the growing number of atheists and agnostics, who portray themselves as some form of intellectual elites and holders of all truth. Often these groups force their views on others, who they propagate must be ignorant to believe in GOD.

We can't ever forget the most significant examples of atheism in action before it became cool in the 2000s. The communist/Marxist Soviet Union and Pol Pot's Cambodia – where millions perished, lives were destroyed, and religion axed as much as they could do. No GOD allowed - yet so much inequality amongst murderous regimes - ruling without freedom of choice for the population, just through fear and persecution.

Everyone has the right to believe whatever they like. However, they must search for the TRUTH and not just accept the untruth because they think it to be accurate based on little more than a 'gut' feeling philosophy or something they read, heard, etc.

There are ABSOLUTE TRUTHS -

The physical world does exist.

Humanity does exist within the physical world.

GOD does exist within the physical and spiritual worlds.

We can experience GOD in so many ways.

GOD is ABSOLUTE LOVE who loves each person equally

Denying GOD because:

> of the evil actions of others,
> or because life isn't fair,
> or because we can't understand suffering,
> or because we can't scientifically prove GOD,
> or because we believe we don't need GOD,
> We see ourselves as so strong that it would be weak to need GOD, etc., is totally wrong!

Denying GOD diminishes our humanity and ability to go beyond ourselves to discover GOD and genuine LOVE.

We need GOD! We need what GOD offers all humanity equally. We need to accept GOD's unconditional love for each one of us!

We need God!

We need what God offers all humanity equally.

We need to accept God's unconditional love for each one of us!

Bryan Foster

Islam Needs a Reformation to End the Violence of its Extremists

Islam is a peaceful religion when followed correctly. No religion can allow a false interpretation of its core scriptures and beliefs to become reality. Violence is not an answer.

Followers of Islam must take direct non-violent action against their extremist followers. There is never any justification for the use of violence in a religious or personal sense. The only somewhat acceptable use of force is when any person is threatened with violence defends themselves with equal force as the attacker. Being careful to not go beyond such force for it to become unjustified, wrong and vindictive.

Using the Koran/Qur'an or other scripture as the basis of Muslims' beliefs, it is important to interpret these correctly.

GOD is against violence. Violence is evil and moves the person away from GOD. Love is becoming destroyed for that person or people through such immoral behaviours.

A major Reforming of Islam's beliefs and practices linked to extremist Muslim followers' violent outcomes is essential for peaceful progress and unity of believers in the only true GOD of all people forever. The same GOD for Islam, Christianity, Hinduism, Judaism and all other legitimate religions and denominations. (Book 1)

We should also not get so caught up with forcing this to happen that the reaction becomes not supported or violent by this believers' section. Those who believe it is their right and is justifiably necessary for Islam's practice today and into the future are wrong. Using the advice from leading Muslims and former

Muslims to bring about the required significant changes is paramount.

People such as former Muslim, politician and academic, Ayaan Ali author of *Heretic: Why Islam Needs A Reformation Now* will be essential leaders of this cause.

Other key people from various religions and cultures who aren't Muslim, will most likely need to be active helpers to achieve the desired peaceful outcomes worldwide.

Ayaan Ali's book is an outstanding literary/religious work. There are also several interviews and conference presentations by Aayan on YouTube, which will help considerably with this Reformation. Due to her unquestionably lived experiences on both sides of the Reformation and Muslim argument, she will help Islam achieve its desired peaceful outcomes.

Throughout this Pre-Reformation and Reformation, we must never lose sight of the fact that Islam, in general, as followed by the majority, is a peaceful, GOD-loving, religion. It is also the second-largest religion worldwide.

Reference: Ayaan Hirst Ali, 2016, *Heretic: Why Islam Needs A Reformation Now,* Fourth Estate (Harper Collins), NY.

Tips for Teachers and Parents to find **GOD** with their Adolescent Students/Children

What are the Essentials Needed to Teach Adolescents about Our Loving GOD?

Being an authentic believer who truly loves GOD and GOD's creations is essential. No pretending about your faith or knowledge will work.

A genuine follower of GOD already has many of the teaching gifts needed.

9 Key areas for successfully teaching/parenting adolescents – 3 personal characteristics + 6 methods.

YOUR:

- Genuine belief in GOD
- Personal and professional lifestyles known by the adolescents - exemplifying GOD's taught lifestyle
- Modelling of your prayer, meditation and sacramental experiences
- Meeting them where they are and lifting them upwards
- Telling your stories about GOD and GOD's encounters with you, e.g. through your prayer or revelation, life stories, etc.
- Being real and honest in your discussions - but always appropriate to the topic and purpose
- Openness to the adolescents about your humanity and its weaknesses and strengths
- Explicit knowledge of GOD and GOD's teachings
- Answering students' questions about GOD.

Love GOD. Live GOD. Fly with GOD!

Teachers and Parents need Passion and Commitment for Adolescents

Teaching is primarily a vocation for those with a passion for espousing the wonder and excitement of learning to our young ones. It is a lot more than just a career. For those who chose to teach as a vocation, this life-long learning/educational experience applies for both students and teachers alike. Through the passion and commitment, the students' best interests come first. It is a journey together with the students. (Yes, we very much need to look after ourselves as well, but a right balance will enable the students to be uppermost in our minds.)

This can even develop for those who 'fell into this teaching career', as long as they develop these attitudes and spiritual beliefs to a high level and then commit to these. You can't pretend, as it becomes quite transparent over time.

Teachers need a lot more than just passion. Anyone can have a particular liking for something important. However, a wholesome appreciation of each student's psychology and cognitive abilities, learning levels and patterns, etc. are necessary. A teacher needs to be fully conversant with their subjects' content and the required pedagogies for brilliant classes. Brilliance in education needs to be a crucial aim for each class, and each lesson.

Two beautiful examples of highly passionate and committed teachers I am honoured to highlight, come from both ends of the education continuum. Gavin has nearly forty years of teaching and leadership experience, and Alice has six years of experience. I have been fortunate to have been one of each person's mentors in their early years. Gavin is currently teaching at a girls' College in Brisbane, where Alice studied as a student. Gavin has also been a Head of Science and Years 11 and 12 Co-ordinator at a brothers' boys' school in Brisbane, HOD Science at another girls' college in Brisbane and Deputy Principal ICT and HOD Science where he now teaches. I taught with Gavin at another girls' college in Brisbane when I was in my late twenties. We were the sports' masters there.

Alice is now at a different girls' college, outside Brisbane after being at Aquinas for her first five teaching years. Alice is primarily a Study of Religion teacher in years 11 and 12.

The characteristics which stand out for both Gavin and Alice is their passion, knowledge, commitment and deep spiritual presence with students and staff alike. Both are genuine, highly informed, trustworthy teachers of exceptional merit. Both are wonderful examples for those fortunate enough to be associated with them in their schools. Gavin and Alice spend many more hours outside of the regular school times involved with extra-curricular activities and all the regular teaching feedback all good teachers pursue, e.g. offering quality feedback through both the drafting and evaluative stages. They are always available for their students throughout the day.

What makes them so exceptional is that all this is done through the love of GOD, adolescents and the genuine vocation of teaching.

Teaching is one profession where you get little feedback in the short term as to your successes. However, in the mid to long term, feedback does often come during departures or special celebrations.

I am so happy to have been of assistance to these two exceptional teachers in their early years of teaching. Teaching truly is a vocation of Love.

Bryan Foster

Show engagement with GOD in prayer

Modelling and properly engaging in our prayer, meditation, and sacramental experiences with our students is essential.

As a teacher of religion, i.e. RE, SOR and R&E, there is no more generous gift to our students than for them to see us fully engaged in our prayer life.

Being seen in contact with GOD is the most liberating and freeing experience for those in our care. It will also initially be a challenge for many students. Particularly for those whose home and life experiences don't exemplify the importance of GOD or prayer.

For our students to see that these necessary aspects of relating to GOD are essential and real for us, they are inspirational.

Authentic, genuine depiction of ourselves in prayer can't be acted/pretended. Students will pick this up quite quickly.

It is often good to maintain a standard classroom format for simplicity of students' preparation and comfort level on most occasions.

Throughout the year, give students various experiences of different prayer types, including spiritual meditation.

When at class, year level, school sacraments/liturgies, we should be the example of closeness to GOD. Expect the best from our students, which develops over time. When they appreciate how important it is for us, they will follow as expected. Don't be the one running around disciplining other class's students. Be the example of prayerfulness. You may need the occasional eye contact discipline though.

Lead each religion class and start each school day with some form of prayer.

Model the standard style. At next prayer time explain the process to be used before doing the prayer as per the described method. As a traditional approach throughout the year, follow the set process.

A classroom prayer example: call for intentions, these could be anything within reason, which students ask for prayer for, including one for the students, which could come from the teacher, e.g. an area of weakness each student decides upon in silence and will pray for silently.

1. Begin the prayer, usually with The Sign of the Cross.

2. Teacher or student leader summarises the intentions like a prayer.

3. Students are asked to pray silently for their intentions.

4. Conclude with a known prayer or one with the words supplied to the students, e.g. the Our Father.

Are Religious Schools Mainly about GOD or Values Education? Or Both?

Pro Deo or Pro Values - For GOD or For Values?

The time is quickly approaching for Australian religious schools and in particular Catholic schools to decide on their main priority – are they here specifically for GOD or just great values. Is the main principle to only be about great pastoral care, an already strong point within Catholic schools, or is GOD the primary reason?

There is a progressing move within Catholic schools to meet the children/students where they and their families are regarding their religiosity. For the great majority, the institutional religion is of minor consequence, if any, these days.

Many parents see the Catholic school as a fantastic place for their children's genuine care. Respect for the individual is high, where their children will get a good quality education and where the fees are reasonable. Initially, it seems to be the right balance between public and private schools' systems. Assuming the private schools have a degree of religious education.

But where is GOD depthed for the Catholic school in this scenario?

A minority even see it as the choice for primary school, but not of real worth for secondary education. For these people, the private secondary schools meet their needs. A good number of these would prefer the old-school-tie and connection-building that occurs there.

The Answer for Catholic Schools?

I would argue that if the fundamental, underlying, essential, belief and basis in the practice of Catholic schooling is not PRO DEO - FOR GOD, then there is no authentic reason for the Catholic school to exist as a Catholic school. If Catholic parents, the governments and community, in general, reject these schools for what they are then a change seems necessary. The other two main options would be that a Catholic school becomes a private, non-governmental religious (but not Catholic) school. Otherwise, it could be changed totally into a state/public school. Obviously, there would be significant problems with many students, families and parishes keen to maintain the traditional first schools in Australia reality.

Many other schools, including many state/public schools, where a robust values-based education is already occurring, is occurring well. To maintain the Catholic school's legitimacy, for this reason, only, would be unnecessary and against most justifications for these schools.

There is no reason whatsoever for the Catholic school to be treated like a cheap, private school or a stepping stone to greater options outside the system, as frequently already occurs, to some degree. There really should be no place for cheap snobbery for those who see it as a better option to public schools and being 'like a private school' but not for religious reasons. Or for the snobs who prefer to keep their 'well-earned' for other reasons and choose a Catholic school over a private school. These last two categories appear to be growing these days.

However, the only reason I believe, which could be argued as valid to maintain the Catholic school as a values-based school without Pro Deo, would be in the belief that the example set by this school could lead to people finding GOD and eventually coming back to, or going to, the Church. However, for me, this is clutching at straws and not an attempt to justify its existence legitimately.

Considering the many options just discussed, is there a final and more fulfilling intelligent option for the Catholic school? Yes, there is! A truly Christ centred Catholic school is BOTH Pro Deo and Pro Values – For God and For Christian and Social Justice Values.

A Catholic school is not a Catholic school:

- Without PRO DEO – without being FOR GOD.
- Without good values and Christian principles and teachings following this initial premise (Pro Deo).
- If GOD and Catholicism are watered down or virtually ignored and is totally against all primary and secondary aims and philosophies of Catholicism.
- If prayers, liturgies, sacraments, meditations and social justice actions, etc., are limited or lost.
- If it doesn't operate, inspire, care for all within its walls in all of the necessary, Catholic school ways how it has done for decades, it can't be a Catholic school. It may have ended up as a Christian school, a secular school, a private school or a state/public school.

Let's Teach Real Religion in Years 7-10

How things have changed in my 40+ years of teaching about GOD to students in secondary schools. I fully appreciate why the changes occurred and at various times was a fully-fledged supporter.

However, I miss the opportunity to teach about GOD properly, without so many impositions and restrictions. Whatever happened to KiS for GOD? Keep it Simple for GOD - and our young people!!!

This article is based on my 40 years of teaching Religious Education/Study of Religion and Religion and Ethics in my retirement year in 2017. And on being a primary/elementary principal and a secondary assistant principal for religious education.

Now we have added a significant piece of assessment each term – to 'be like all the other subjects and give Religious Education credibility'. If parents and administrators knew how much time went on assessment and preparing the students for great results, I think they would agree with me – no more major assessment in years 7-10!!! It wastes so much time, and for what? To show that this content about GOD is real and vital and should be treated as seriously as all the other subjects. Really?!

How about this proposal? It is far more critical than any other subject. Each child's salvation and life is assisted so much by it! When will the western world realise that GOD is central to everything? That we need to have a healthy, loving relationship with GOD. That there are no free tickets to Heaven!

I am not against a smaller, minimalistic approach to assessment.

The continual observations of students and their responses and input, Q and As for students and by students, workshops and other activities etc., could all form the assessment necessity, if accepted by those in power. These forms allow for so much freedom needed to learn about, and experience, GOD!

In the educational system where I was a full-time teacher and leader, there are 30 minutes a day set aside for specific Religious Education. This 30 minutes is in addition to the required teaching time for all secular subjects, as dictated by the state government educational authorities. It is a bonus for Catholic schools! This doesn't happen in government schools and most other independent schools. All the different literary and numeric skills etc. are supposed to occur in the other 5 hours per day. RE's time is additional and should allow for pure RE and not be expected to add another layer of literacy and numeracy etc. development. Even though this would occur incidentally during this RE time.

How unique is this? What an opportunity for GOD to become one with us in unimaginable ways? Yet, teaching is then divided amongst the other apparently 'necessary' addition of assessment. Assessment is present for a few primary reasons: firstly, to give the subject credibility and a perceived equal partnership with the other secular subjects; secondly, it is supposed to get the attention of the students who wouldn't see it as anything but unimportant without having a significant piece of assessment; thirdly, it helps the insecure or religiously uneducated teacher to hold on to something that can take up so much of their class time that it becomes a security blanket. More and more teachers in my system are unprepared or uneducated to teach Religious Education or Religion and Ethics (and in some instances, Study of Religion, which counts towards their senior certificate and university entrance score).

If it is so difficult to get qualified teachers into this subject department, that assessment is necessary, so be it! This should occur compared to nothing at all.

However, for people like myself, who have been teaching this subject for many years, there should be an opportunity to be FREE for GOD in the time and topics given. Students very much enjoy qualified and interested teachers to teach any subject, but particularly religion. If this is the case, it provides a solid argument for no major RE assessment but some previously mentioned, smaller options. To teach the content required by the syllabus/program but not to have to be restricted by assessment, (possibly, unless this is an option chosen by the individual teacher). To be free to go to places rarely seen in the educational sphere. To truly depth each student's appreciation of, and relationship with, GOD!

I can be reasonably confident that my method resonates with virtually most of my students over the years. My students very much love the subject and the content being taught and how it was being taught. They were engaged and are learning to love GOD and GOD's messages for us. I would also suspect that their personal and family relationships are becoming more assertive due to their appreciation of GOD and GOD's espoused values and teachings.

You know, I don't think Jesus, Moses, Mohammad, St Peter, St Thomas Aquinas, or any other significant religious leader, had ASSESSMENT on the scale we have now in years 7-10! Any ideas why??? Because it isn't needed! It isn't required, as a part of learning about or experiencing GOD! Qualified RE teachers are needed much more than significant assessment items.

Postscript (2017): I have just introduced this term's assessment and guess what? STOP! A whole new tact has occurred this week. Everyone, students and myself alike, are now in assessment mode. There is a palpable difference in atmosphere and classroom expectations. Now students want to know what they have to do to achieve their best result! They will learn considerable content on their topic. But everything has now become focused on results!!! The freedom to discover GOD has gone. The freedom to engage on various levels, both subjective and objective is now so much more limited.

Just this week, due to time constraints, I couldn't answer a very good, but not relevant to the assignment question. As we are now in assessment mode, taking most of the lesson on an 'irrelevant' question isn't possible. As this isn't a rare occasion, you can imagine the difficulty when the assessment has such importance and priority, no matter what certain people say.

Freedom to teach GOD in the best ways possible does not require a significant piece of assessment each term in years 7-10.

(Edited Extract - article from 2017 by Bryan Foster.)

Author's 42 years Teaching Religion

Author's 40 years of Catholic Education Celebrated on World Teachers Day

I was fortunate to celebrate my 40 years of teaching in Catholic schools a couple of years ago, once at a Brisbane Catholic Education lunch and yesterday at my school where I have taught for the past 28 years…

Work and career help us all find meaning and even at times, love. Love of colleagues, managers, etc. Not a couple's love but colleagues and fellow worker's love. Work's income helps us survive, and have the finances needed for life.

Whatever you try to achieve at the beginning of your working life, try to do for a career, give yourself life-affirming and enjoyable work opportunities. Search far and wide, if necessary. There isn't anything worth doing unless you enjoy its challenges, purpose, benefit to others, etc. Once you select your first direction in life, aim for success, enjoyment, reward for yourself and others. But make sure it's something you'll benefit from and enjoy each working day. As time continues, you'll see what direction in life is best for you. Don't be afraid to change careers, if the one you're doing isn't to your liking or reward, etc.

Wow! How exciting to be able to celebrate with you, on this World Teachers Day, 40 years of teaching in Catholic schools. Especially my 27 years teaching at Aquinas, and my eight years here as a student, from year 5 to 12.

Aquinas is very special to me. Thirty-five years of direct involvement has had a considerable impact on me, as well as on my family. Many of you are already aware that my three children graduated from here, two are Catholic school teachers, one in Australia and the other in Canada. My wife, Karen, also teaches at St Kevin's. Our youngest daughter is studying Science at UQ.

Teaching is a gratifying yet challenging vocation. Some of my best life experiences happened during my time as a teacher. Many opportunities also came my way. I would invite everyone interested in helping young people be the best they can be in a challenging world and consider this profession a genuine option for your career. Ignore a large amount of criticism this option seems to attract from many sources. Good teachers are an essential basis of a thriving community.

I want to thank the Catholic Church, and in particular, the Brisbane and Toowoomba Catholic Education offices, for so many beautiful opportunities and experiences given over the past 55 years, since my first communion:

Primary and secondary education at Guardian Angels and Aquinas

Tertiary education at McAuley Teachers College and the Australian Catholic University in Brisbane and Sydney

Teaching at: Aquinas and Marymount on the GC, MacKillop and Seton Colleges and St Bernard's in Brisbane, St Mary's Goondiwindi and St Joseph's Tara.

Leadership positions of Assistant Principal RE, Years 11 and 12 Coordinator (like the Pastoral Leaders but on a year level arrangement), and Marketing Manager at Aquinas, Sports Master at MacKillop in Brisbane and Principal of 2 country primary schools.

Over the past ten years while at Aquinas, I enjoyed writing some books in my spare time. These were on marketing schools and churches, along with last year's book on GOD. Some of you may even know about my travel and caravan videos on YouTube.

I would especially like to thank so many of you sitting here today, and many more students who have graduated over the past 40 years, especially allowing me to teach you about GOD, Jesus, world religions, ethics and spirituality. These fundamental aspects of our lives are becoming more lost in our world today. Could I strongly suggest that these will always be very important, no matter how insignificant some people seem to place each? GOD is real. GOD loves you so much. Love GOD.

Thank you too for walking, running, resting, even hiding at times with me, or from me on this education journey we are all on to the wonderful leadership teams and teaching and ancillary staff. I feel truly blessed to have had so many tops of the field mentors and supporters over such a long period.

Thank you, everyone, for putting up with me, yet still being with, travelling with, and supporting me. I could not have done this without so many very special people.

Thank you to my parents, who have helped me so much. I strongly suggest that you listen to your parents, carers and other significant family members for advice and support. And most importantly, a huge thank you to my most loving wife, Karen. The love of my life and mother of our children, and the grandmother of our grandchildren. We will have been married 40 years next year. Karen has always encouraged, supported and challenged me both personally and professionally. I am who I am because of Karen.

Enjoy your time here at Aquinas. Aquinas is an exceptional college which genuinely has your best interests at heart. Accept the challenges and opportunities offered. Work hard and ask questions. You have an exceptional leadership team, teaching and ancillary staff and parents and friends association. Use these incredible resources to your advantage.

Thank you so much for allowing me to offer these thoughts this morning. Just as St Paul said in the reading read by Mr Alexander

(APRE), "For we are GOD's servants, working together; you are GOD's field, GOD's building." I invite you to love education as much as I have. To be GOD's field being open to GOD, building something extraordinary and unique within each one of you.

Education is power. Power enables opportunities for you and others. Use your passion and education to help make our world a better place for EVERYONE.

(Edited extracts from Bryan's 40th-year school assembly address. Copyright 2017 – Bryan Foster)

Retirement - Life's Journey Takes Another Direction

Most teachers have a real love and passion for teaching. A genuine Love of their students. And a desire to be the best teacher and role model they can be.

It has been an absolute pleasure to have taught in Catholic education for 40 years. Retirement from full-time teaching is a sad yet necessary decision. Special thanks to all involved over so many years for your encouragement, challenges and support. I believe that this genuinely noble vocation has so enhanced me that it is easy to let go and let GOD continue to take me forward on my journey. This closes 55 years of full-time Catholic school involvement.

I would like to thank Brisbane Catholic Education, Toowoomba Catholic Education and Corpus Christi College for giving me so many years of unforgettable, life-enriching experiences + one fantastic wife. Karen and I attended McAuley College together and married the year Karen graduated. Our three children were educated in exceptional Catholic schools. Two have become teachers - Leigh-Maree is at GA and Andrew in Canada. Jacqui is studying Science at UQ. Our two grandchildren have recently begun their journey likewise.

Being a Religious Education specialist has undoubtedly added to my religious and spiritual journeys towards and with GOD. All my qualifications were RE centred, especially: the Dip RE from the then newly created Institute of Faith Education, the BEd and Grad Dip RE from McAuley College and the MEd (RE) from ACU Sydney.

Being the first male principal who graduated from McAuley College entertained me no end (but was hardly significant really in the scheme of things). I thank Toowoomba Catholic Education for the opportunity to be a school principal at Tara and Goondiwindi. These were challenging yet enriching times. None of this would have eventuated without the outstanding teacher training McAuley College offered, along with some exceptional mentoring from my first schools' teachers, principals from BCE and staff from within the Toowoomba CEO.

Developing my APRE role to include marketing a Catholic college from 1994 until 2009 at Aquinas was unique and fulfilling. To learn and discover on the spot and to work closely with the small, newly formed marketing unit within BCE was a significant move into a different field for me but once again thoroughly enjoyable and rewarding. Six months in the BCE 'Catching Fire' unit with Jill Goudie, helped depth so much of my life, relationships and broader skills. These all led to writing school and church marketing books with the final two of the five editions published in 2011: 'School Marketing Manual for the Digital Age (3rd ed)' and the 'Church Marketing Manual for the Digital Age (2nd ed)'.

After 30 years teaching Study of Religion to years 11 to 12 and 40 years teaching Religious Education overall to all year levels from years 1 to 12, along with some profound professional and personal relationships with specific family, school, parish and Brisbane Catholic Education staff and clergy, and various friends, I have been extremely fortunate to have developed a unique and strong relationship with GOD.

In 2016, I wrote and published the first book in the *'GOD Today'* (Eight books' series) *Series - '1GOD.world: One GOD for All: A Discovery of GOD and GOD's Messages for Today's World'*. This Book 6, which you are now reading, was published five years later in 2021 - *Love is the Meaning of Life: GOD's Love*.

Twenty-eight years at my alma mater, Aquinas College, as a teacher, APRE and Years 11/12 Coordinator has been quite remarkable. My days as a student from year 5-12, were indirectly accentuated with personal development in leadership - mainly through sport, risk-taking, becoming a 'Catholic Gentleman' and boldness.

Thank you to my educational communities, friends and family for so much that will remain with me forever.

For the future, plans include writing the remainder of this *'GOD Today' Series* over the next year or two and returning to making YouTube *GOD Today*, caravan and travel videos for my 'efozz1' channel. I'm sure there will be some caravanning there also!

As I discovered after retiring, a critical aspect of retirement is preparing for the massive lifestyle change. I suggest strongly that you have thought long and hard about this move and be well on the road learning and preparing for the challenging change. Part-time volunteering is especially rewarding for many people. Apart from the financial aspects of retirement, is the significant increase in time available to you. In some ways, time means money and your ability to manage your finances is critical. For most people, when they see their superannuation total, all they can see is spend, spend, spend! Don't do this, until you and your financial planner, have set up your pension plan with your superannuation fund and your governmental pension arrangements (if over a certain age)!!! Forget about the new, so-called 'smaller' house to build, the best new large caravan to put in the specially constructed carport of your new home, the overseas trips and cruisers to share, the payments to your children to help them be debt-free, etc. etc. etc.

Spend wisely. Engage a good financial planner to work with you to gain the best opportunities for you. Your superannuation fund should be able to help you find this person or have one available for you. Your bank can also point you in the right direction – possibly to their people if this suits you. Check around with friends for a good planner they know or recommend through friends, work, etc. Consider all the ramifications of 'throwing' your money away or giving it uncontrollably to authentic, worthwhile causes.

Take time deciding. Some people find it useful to start small at first. Restraint in spending is essential. Of course, spend it wisely on what will help you genuinely relax and move to create and become part of the 'grey-nomad crew' or professional groups for retirees, church groups, men's or ladies' clubs, card clubs, gyms, sports' clubs etc. Others may continue doing similar work to which they were doing before retirement. Many people become consultants in their fields of expertise. This is good but beware of its financial impact (and taxation, if any?) on your pension, if any, when you decide to move to that.

I changed significantly from religion teacher of 42 years to book author part-time from 2008. I retired in 2017. This *'GOD Today' Series* began in 2016. This was a slow path to where I am. I plan to continue writing when I can timewise and with the correct affordability. Writing is gratifying and enjoyable for those who are interested. Beware, there isn't much income unless you are a best seller.

Your financial planner's expertise should play a key role in your decisions. Remember your superannuation, which possibly by now has become, or will soon become, part of your private, self-funded pension plan, has to last a couple of decades for many people. Most people will be able to mix their pension when transferred from their superannuation fund with the government's public pension at some time after retirement. (Check government policies.) This governmental pension is a pension provided by your federal government to assist you after work finishes. You reach a certain age depending on when you were born, as another part of your income. It is something you have worked for most of your working life. Your balance will also help you get into an aged care facility when eventually needed. The governmental pension, in most countries, is available until your death.

Conclusion

The great majority of the human population needs and craves to be in love. It is one of those most special gifts from GOD for each of us to share throughout our world. We have just explored so many aspects of love in this book, from the incredibly extraordinary, i.e. absolute divine love from GOD; down to humans loving differently with various people, animals or animistic possessions or objects or lifestyles or power or wealth, etc., but most importantly, GOD and Humanity overall.

The whole appreciation of true LOVE comes from GOD to us so that we know we need love and subsequently work to achieve that unique state of being in love with those whom we spend our lives. Genuine, wholesome, enhancing, personal and communal love, is what makes us truly, and fully, human.

People react differently to each other in various loving relationships. Love has different levels for different relationships, e.g. GOD, Family relationships, friendships, objects, etc. Our love would be at different levels depending on the life circumstances, personalities, genuineness of spouse, partner, children, other family members or friends relationships, etc.

Unfortunately, some people try to 'buy' love from others. Or try to force others to love them or someone else. Or actually, even blackmail and abuse some for their benefit and not for the one/s who they are approaching for 'love'. This is not what love is. Some people even let their physical attractions and urges dominate the whole relationship. This is bad, but it could also be a so evil, inhumane, selfish, person, looking for 'love' (often it is just lust) but not being successful. Be very careful of these types of people.

As loving humans, it is our duty and privilege to consider all the people with whom we come in contact. We all gain from positive human relationships. These are integral to a healthy human lifestyle and necessary for Love - to take a vital place in each of our lives. We all must learn from our mistakes with ourselves and others and act accordingly. Always remember that GOD is on your side. Keep in close contact seeking assistance, strength, compassion, forgiveness, etc. GOD will be the most effective helper when times get tough. Just call on GOD for help and 'listen' inwardly to the suggestions, often coming to you as thoughts, inspirations and support.

GOD listens to our prayers and reacts in whatever way GOD decides is best for us. Accept this and work towards some helpful and fulfilling ideas, thoughts, lifestyle enjoyments, happiness, etc. GOD doesn't always answer our prayers in the way we would like or expect. That is very much acceptable, though. GOD wants the best for each of us, so trust in the various solutions and suggestions offered by GOD, who is the answer now or is the start of a response coming to you over time.

The significant challenge offered in this book revolves around all living things, except humanity, being treated equally by God, no matter whether animal or plant. Due to their superiority, humans are treated at a higher level than the other lifeforms. Their advanced spiritual, physical, emotional, and psychological powers etc. place them in critical positions for soul-filled decisions on life and our world. These are beyond any other flora or fauna capacity.

GOD's Absolute Love for all soul-filled living entities helps explain the absolute meaning of life for all. Our prayerful relationship with GOD is critical for our salvation. GOD's Love surrounds us permanently. We have to build on this day after day until we reach our salvation with GOD after our Earthly death.

There are several religious love challenges for us today. Our personal and communal justice for all people and lifeforms is essential for a LOVING world shared together. Social media and various digital media platforms have multiple responsibilities for the treatment of people worldwide. If these groups aren't enhancing the population as a whole, then their power is being misused, and various people may be harmed.

As believers of God, Church, equality, etc., we are comforted to find various solutions to these aforementioned love challenges above. These religious Love solutions are considered in depth.

Appendix 1

Where it all began – Author's 25th Birthday Revelation

The day doubt disappeared, and my faith journey went to an unimagined higher level. On this day, I gained a whole new perspective of GOD and GOD's part in my life. Tears from GOD's love were experienced for the first time. The doubt about the reality of GOD disappeared. 'Let Go and Let GOD' became an actual spiritual reality of a profound order.

The stars all seemed to have aligned. It was my 25th birthday. As well as the school's uniquely offered, annual 'Commitment Day'. It was also my last day at this school. At the end of the day, I left this school for my first country school principalship – which began on the Monday after leaving Brisbane.

It started with birthday excitement, but the last day of school sadness and ended in tears of absolute joy and oneness with GOD.

This school was unique in its philosophy and enrolment policy. One key difference to most schools was its strong association with the charismatic Catholic movement. This was especially manifested in the annual 'Commitment Day' to GOD. Various staff had unique GOD gifts, which they actively used within the charismatic movement, but are not limited to this movement. Many people have these multiple gifts from GOD but often aren't aware of such gifts. The other common one is Speaking in Tongues, which I have witnessed on many occasions. On this day, the seven teachers with the charismatic gift of healing were engaged for much of the time healing students and teachers alike.

This healing encompasses any weaknesses we have, e.g. physical, emotional or social.

On this day the students and staff of this junior secondary Brisbane Catholic school began the day with a special Mass celebrated by a charismatic priest from Melbourne. The mass was followed by invitation to students and staff to commit to GOD sometime throughout the day. There was no compulsion, though. The students could roam the school freely throughout the day with the only prerequisite being no noise near the church. Staff supervised.

The staff of fourteen had seven charismatic teachers who had the spiritual gift of healing. The principal was a sister in a religious order—many of these charismatic teachers, plus the priest, present at various church positions throughout the day. Students could choose who they would like to pray with when offering their commitment to GOD. Most stations would have many students continue with the staff member.

I sat with a particular student during the mass. This student was in a few of my classes. It took about an hour after mass concluded for this student to ask me to accompany her to pray with the principal and her present group of students. It was quite an event to go through the process to get there, due to various circumstances. However, once there, we were invited by the principal to move to the front of her group of eighteen to twenty students. Sister asked this student if she would like us to pray for her. She then asked me if I'd like to place my hand on the student's shoulder and pray. I agreed and prayed for her from very deep within my heart and soul - no speaking in tongues, just everyday English.

This belief in prayer causing healing, however, had caused me significant challenges that morning. I was tearing myself apart inside through the doubt that enveloped me about the whole healing circumstances that had been occurring in the church that past hour. Not being a charismatic person myself and having significant doubts about the entire healing process through a person being prayed over action, caused me significant concerns. Much of this doubt was based on the television evangelists we would see on Sunday morning television back in the 1970s and 1980s where people were miraculously 'healed' in large numbers before our very eyes as if this was the norm. There was truth to many of these healings, yet there was always so much doubt, as well. It was remembering that many of these tele-evangelists eventually admitted to fraud or other inappropriate behaviours. I had also witnessed charismatics healing at a local Brisbane parish while eighteen years of age and at teachers' college. This had impressed me enough to want to consider it more. The tele-evangelists over the previous years up until this Commitment Day made belief in this healing process very difficult indeed.

So, as I walked this young lady to Sister, I was in incredible anguish internally. I was fighting against the possibility of something extraordinary. Each group had crying or sniffling people, and all were arm in arm with each other. It seemed to be too much for this doubter. Once I was asked by Sister to pray for the young lady, I instantly decided to 'Let Go and Let GOD'. This freeing moment was something quite unbelievable in itself. The confusion and doubt turned to belief and love. Sister then placed her hands on the girl's head and prayed. At that moment, the student broke down and tears freely flowed. I was now also tear-filled.

Next Sister asked if I'd like her to pray over me. What followed was life-changing. As she placed her hands on my head and prayed, there was this incredible feeling of heat flow from my head downwards to my feet. I then broke down and cried tears of absolute love for GOD and those around me. *This is the moment in time that all my confusion, doubts and challenges about GOD disappeared.*

Later that afternoon, I asked Sister what had happened, and she explained that GOD came into me and that my old self was 'washed away' (downwards) and that I was 'filled up' with the new me.

I have remained so faith-filled and full of GOD's oneness and awe ever since – that is 36 years. My faith has never wavered since that day; even when some very challenging issues have confronted me. GOD was with me through each of these.

That was the day I truly learned that tears in specific instances are a sign from GOD - that GOD is truly present at that particular moment.

I am often asked if a similar experience of how GOD came to me, along with the Tears from GOD, will happen to others, to my students, their families and friends, my colleagues, etc. I genuinely believe that it could if the opportunity availed itself. We need to accept GOD's offer, whenever and wherever made. We may need to search out the possibilities. We may not expect it when it does happen. I believe the secret is always to be open to receiving GOD in both expected and unexpected ways. GOD loves us beyond our imagining and wants the best for each of us. We must not be blinded to GOD by all the distractions of this world. We need to be prepared for GOD to come in whatever way GOD chooses. It may not be what we expect, though.

We need to clear our minds and hearts to the beauty, purity and awesomeness that is GOD. We need stillness, openness and desire to accept whatever GOD offers, whenever GOD provides it.

The notion in much of the western world today is that we don't need GOD. It is either because we have so much or because we are blinded by so much - which is an absolute fallacy.

We need GOD as much today if not more as in any time and at any place in history have needed GOD.

It is the first significant time in history that the belief in GOD and acceptance of GOD being with us on this earth is diminishing. It is a time of absolute urgency requiring a major cultural shift towards GOD and GOD's people here today.

> ...there was this incredible feeling of heat flow from my head downwards to my feet.
>
> I then broke down and cried Tears from God - of absolute love for God and those around me.
>
> *This is the moment in time that all my confusion, doubts and challenges about God disappeared.*

(Edited Extract from *Where's GOD? Revelations Today*, 2018, by Bryan Foster, p131-135)

Appendix 2

Mt Warning – Word of GOD Revelation – the Story

In 2016 GOD 'came down' from the mountain. This most majestic Australian 'mountain' in the Northern Rivers, NSW, and offered forth a most remarkable experience of GOD for the author. Having just spent three days touring around Mt Warning, reflecting on it, photographing and videoing it and staying in a caravan/trailer park on its plain, all was to culminate in a nighttime oneness with GOD event. This Revelation moment is indelibly etched on my whole being.

I had the most remarkable opportunity to experience GOD's Word firsthand, literally. I had taken leave to recuperate from illness and stayed for a few days in a caravan in my wife's original hometown. The campsite I chose significantly had a view of Mt Warning in the background. A 'mountain' I had viewed thousands of times over the years, mainly since I was 18 and had met my future wife and her local farming family. Mt Warning is an imposing 'mountain' feature in the far north of New South Wales, Australia. I say mountain, in reality, it isn't in any comparative height-sense like the mountains of Europe/Asia or the Americas. For the oldest continent, Australia, it is quite imposing. Being a volcanic core, it stands out literally within the caldera features of a vast ancient volcano. The shape is very appealing and attractive. Its centrality within the region causes it to be a feature admired from all directions.

Over three days, I drove the 72km around its base and up to the walkers' departure point (on bitumen and gravel roads). Around sugar cane farms and through national parks and small villages, I videoed and photographed it from all possible directions, sat and reflected with it, observed it, drove and walked to crucial observation points, visited its base, and became very familiar with it. You could almost say, I became one with it.

On the third day, I was awoken at night. I was very aware of my breathing and of breathing cold, fresh, clean air. I just lay there breathing deeply in through the nose, holding each breath for a couple of seconds and slowly blowing it out through the mouth. There was a real sense of presence. I started to realise it was quite a cold night and that I was lying at the foot of Mt Warning, relatively. I began to get this powerful awareness that I was one with the mountain. The mountain and I had grown together significantly these past three days, and now we were at a climax. The Truth would become apparent.

I then started to get a message to write down what I was about to receive. And to be very accurate.

I soon realised that, just as in ancient times, the mountain was a conduit to GOD. Prophets from many religions had climbed mountains to be closer to GOD and received GOD's message for that time and place in history and often for subsequent eras. I was not to climb the mountain tonight. (Or ever again due to an injury.) But I was to climb it figuratively.

Or was it a case of GOD coming down from the mountain?

Remarkably, what followed blew me away! Without thinking about what I was to write, I found myself writing down a list of instructions, teachings, and refreshers. Was it truly from GOD? It sure felt like it. But how could I tell? I was told within my mind not to overthink this; to go with the flow - that it was all legitimate and would become apparent as the night went on. The challenge for me was that since my 25th birthday religious experience (See 25th birthday story in Appendix 1), tears were a sign for me of

GOD's presence, the greater the tears, the greater the divine presence. (See 'Tears from GOD')

Yet, there were no tears tonight. But there was ecstasy and a realisation of what was happening. A font of wisdom was unfolding, and I was so, fortunately, a part of it. The list was completed. An explanation from me of what had occurred was recorded after the list. (See 'Revelation Notes' after the 'GOD's 12 Revelations' section.) And a perfect sleep followed.

The next morning was a Sunday, and I attended the Catholic sacrament/ritual of the Eucharist in the church in which Karen and I were married forty years ago this year! The mass was by coincidence a First Communion Mass for the local Catholic school. During the Mass, I asked GOD if what happened last night was real – what followed was an outpouring of tears. The answer was an emphatic, "Yes!"

> I then started to get a message to write down what I was about to receive…
>
> I soon began to realise that, just as in ancient times, the mountain was a conduit to God.

(Edited Extract from *Where's GOD? Revelations Today*, 2018, by Bryan Foster, p58-60)

Appendix 3

What are Revelations and Inspired Messages from GOD?

This book refers to Revelations as those inspired messages coming directly from GOD through a unique encounter with GOD and the person receiving them. However, there should also be some form of 'proof' of this reality, such as Tears from GOD and other justification points (explained shortly) before it is entirely accepted and shared as the Truth. Inspired messages are those thoughts and issues received through prayerful experiences or other people, nature or events -from wherever GOD is inspiring us. However, a process of discernment is needed to clarify the authenticity of these and is different from ordinary thoughts and feelings.

The concept of 'Revelations' in this book are also referred to as 'Special or Direct Revelations' in various religious circles in society. GOD specifically directs these Revelations to individuals or groups. What is referred to as 'inspired messages' in this publication may, at times, be referred to as 'General Revelations' in other religious publications and discussions? These are from GOD to anyone in general, being received through such means as nature, ethical appreciations and cognitive reasoning. (GCSE, BBC) Christianity believes that Jesus is the ultimate example of Revelation's fullness on this earth by humanity. (Oxford Scholarship, 2018) The different religions have various appreciations of the relevance of Revelations historically and today. All genuine religions believe that GOD reveals GODself to this world through various forms, especially through people, their beliefs and morality, and the natural world.

The terms 'Revelation' and 'inspired messages' are used as points of clarity. Naming every message with which GOD inspires humanity with the word 'Revelation' may become confusing as there are different Revelation levels. 'Revelation' is used when there is direct contact of GOD with specific people, while 'inspired messages' are for those revelations discerned by people as emanating from GOD. How both of these occur is explained.

This book is primarily about explaining the various Revelations I received directly from GOD in 1982, 2016 and 2018, along with GOD's inspired messages and discerned over more than thirty-five years. There is an inherent, authentic sense of the Truth being shared.

The literary style states the Revelations and inspired messages received or discerned from GOD accurately without diminishing each through diplomatic, political or politically correct forms.

The key Revelations and inspired messages will be stated clearly and without a softening or hardening to appease certain groups who may not fully or partially agree with each statement. Each Revelation and inspired message will be explained in enough detail to make the point succinctly and clearly.

There is a real emphasis on Keeping it Simple for GOD's People. Too often religious preachers, teachers and theologians emphasise too much detail beyond the clarity of the message. People then get lost in all the detail, and the point from GOD is missed. This book aims to keep the messages simple yet explained with enough detail to gain a proper understanding.

This book is not an apologetic work. It is not teaching or preaching a set of one religion's doctrines over another religion's. It is not standing up and fighting for any particular religion or religious leader or any specific belief or faith patterns from any specific religion.

It is a book of the Truth about and basically from the forever One and Only GOD of existence.

All genuine religions are equal and have an essential role from GOD for each of their followers. The belief in only one GOD is most liberating and beneficial for appreciating and following GOD.

This truth is the Truth of GOD for today's global and interconnected world. The following section explains why I make this claim.

It has been quite a journey to get to this point. It began in 1982 when receiving the Tears from GOD, and physical warmth flowing from head to foot received as part of the gift of healing from Sister Ann at a secondary school's Commitment Day. Over the interim period from 1982 until now so much has been discerned as GOD's inspired messages. This discernment process is explained.

After receiving GOD's Revelation in 2016, explained in various ways and sections throughout the book, the initial reaction was one of doubt - even though there were many Tears from GOD on many occasions privately and with my wife, Karen, to show its authenticity and genuineness.

When it came to the crunch to decide what would be highlighted in the first book in this *'GOD Today' Series*, *1GOD.world: One GOD for All*, I wasn't able to run with all the Revelations. I was only able to highlight the 'One GOD only – One GOD' Revelation and some subsequent discerned inspired messages from GOD and stories of experiencing GOD throughout my life. A real doubting Thomas scenario occurred. In hindsight, I now believe this was all part of GOD's plan. GOD initially wanted me to highlight the One GOD Only Revelation, along with the messages and stories contained in that edition.

This approach used for the first book in this *'GOD Today' Series* opened up the opportunities for me to grow into the other Revelations this past couple of years and to discern a better appreciation of each. To also gain the courage to go out into the world and state these with authority. It wasn't just a matter of listing these but to believe strongly in each one and explain each one in detail. GOD wanted these Revelations to become part of the world's meaningful and fully understood lexicon.

We all need to appreciate these Revelations and what these mean so that we can each make the Revelations an integral part of our lives.

Hence, this second book is written with a higher level of understanding and appreciation than the previous edition. It includes so much more on both the Revelations from 1982 and 2016 and the original and subsequent inspired GOD messages.

(Edited Extract from *Where's GOD? Revelations Today*, 2018, by Bryan Foster, p35-38)

Appendix 4

Are the Revelations and inspired messages contained in this series the Truth from God?

As an author, extolling the Revelations and inspired messages from God is a most challenging task. It goes well beyond just writing some thoughts and meanings. It goes to the whole core of appreciating ourselves and humanity and our association with God. To claim the authority to do so is a massive personal challenge. Rest assured it hasn't been done lightly. In fact, there is considerable truly heartfelt anxiety. In my heart of hearts, I genuinely believe in everything written in this publication wholeheartedly.

The collection is one author's Revelations and inspired messages from God. Others throughout the world are also receiving Revelations and inspired messages. Some will probably put these into publications. We all have our ways of dealing with and propagating what we receive. All people can receive God's messages and Revelations. The big question for each person is, Am I ready and open to receiving messages or Revelations from God? Would I know when I received any? What would I do with these if and when I had similar experiences? God inspires us in so many ways, mainly through other people and nature. Am I aware of inspired messages from God through others and our world?

These Revelations and inspired messages revealed to me have been developing over at least forty years. It is not something which has just eventuated.

The critical reasons for believing that these Revelations and inspired messages are from God and explained in more detail. The detail of each follows the specific reasons.

- the 25th birthday experience and Revelation of God in May 1982;
- the Tears from God experiences, which have been growing in intensity and frequency, especially in the most recent years;
- the longevity without any personal doubt of this strong association with God;
- the Revelations from God at the foot of Mt Warning in May 2016 and November 2018;
- the recent photographic images highlighting metaphorical or direct links with God;
- coincidences and signs from God over many years
- the personal career/vocation, 40 years teaching religion from years 1-12, including 30 years of Study of Religion to senior years;
- holding senior leadership positions in religious schools and parishes;
- prayer and meditation throughout and
- the continued strong support and agreement from my wife, Karen.

Each of these reasons supports the belief in either the Revelation or inspired messages being from God. God never forces anyone to believe anything. There is a level of 'proof' but also the mystery of the faith with any Revelation or inspired message from God. Therefore, through the combinations of these reasons and others, God's unique presence is experienced with the outcomes of each needed to be shared. Having always been close to God, or at least in my teens on the fringes, allows for that openness to hear and know intrinsically when something is legitimately from God.

The 25th birthday experience is explained in detail in Appendix 7. The longevity of living without any doubt about God since that 25th birthday experience is quite significant. Since that 1982 experience when God extraordinarily came to me when prayed over by a charismatic religious sister who also had a masters degree in psychology, there has been absolutely no doubt about God's existence or God's absolute equal love for each human person throughout history. This 1982 revelatory moment was when I first truly experienced Tears from God in such depth. It also included the incredible warmth flowing from Sister's hands placed on the top of my head downwards through my whole body.

From that moment, over thirty-five years ago, there have been some tough and challenging times, as there are for everyone over their lifetimes. For me, these were mainly of personal health and financial types. Some were life-threatening or life-changing beyond any expectation or plan. There was also the everyday life challenging experiences of others. These range from family to the global. The global challenges needing to be worked-through include war, poverty and other injustices throughout the world and God's place with all these. Then there are the direct challenges in your beliefs, particularly from atheists. Members of this group are becoming particularly vicious and hate-filled towards anyone who espouses faith in God. This was experienced directly when I opened myself up to various religious sites on social media.

The Tears from God experiences have been growing in intensity and regularity in recent years. These were initially experienced in 'introductory' levels from about fifteen in year ten when I first wondered if I would like to join the priesthood to a higher level while at College in my late teenage years. One significant and influential event while at College was visiting a Sunday night charismatic mass where people were being healed through the Holy Spirit. The 25th birthday moment was the first significant Tears from God moment for me. Since then, similar sorts of occasions have been potent and enhancing. Each shows those extraordinary moments of pure bliss and the presence of God. The Tears from God are the primary means of knowing God's unique presence and occasion of confirming those Revelations or inspired messages. (See 'Tears from God' - the following section.)

In 2016 at the foot of Mt Warning, I was awoken and told by God in my mind's eye to write down precisely as God sent me the Revelations. (The early morning encounter with God is explained in detail shortly in the 'Mt Warning...' story. See Appendix 2.) This supernatural Revelation was confirmed the following morning at a First Communion Mass in the church where I was married forty-three years ago this year – through a Tears from God moment. Once again, two years later, more Revelations occurred at the foot of Mt Warning. These are those numbered sixteen to twenty-one.

There have been some different experiences, often recorded as photographs, which seem to show God telling a story or offering a particular message. This message may be metaphorical or literal. Often it is God giving a sign of support, or confirmation of that specific message. A point of encouragement to the message's authenticity and the need for it to be shared with others. In my particular case, the need to accept my place in the scheme of God's plan and to go and do whatever is required to propagate the Revelation or message!

There is one photo taken by my wife, Karen, inside St Peter's Basilica in Rome in 2007. It has a stream of light shining down from the ceiling window onto me only! Nothing was read into this until this year. This year there have been five quite similar sunlight events to each other, in close time proximity. One occurred at the foot of Mt Warning just after sunrise; another at Texas on the NSW/Queensland border; a third was at Straddie, North Stradbroke Island.

In contrast, another two occurred at Kingscliff and Cabarita in northern New South Wales, close to Mt Warning, Australia. These encounters have been explained in detail in this first section of the book. I believe that these images are part of the overall methods God uses to make particular points. These are just one method of many.

Coincidences often point to special moments. In Part 2 of *Where's God? Revelations Today* these are explored along with previously mentioned various sunlight experiences in signs and coincidences.

The chosen career/vocation choice to teach and specialise in teaching religion eventuated forty-two years of teaching religion in religious schools. Needing, but also strongly desiring, to daily start each school day and each religious lesson with some communication with God is incredibly empowering. Class prayer and meditation was highly significant for all these years. For thirty of these years, the academic Study of Religion classes for years eleven and twelve required both the spiritual dimension and the academic dimension. This subject needed an intimate knowledge and considerable experience of Christianity, Islam, Judaism, Buddhism, Hinduism and Australian Aboriginal Spirituality. Teaching religion on these various levels every working day for such an extended time develops a genuine spiritual relationship with God. Your day is so much God-based. You truly get to appreciate God from each religion's perspectives and beliefs. Combine this with your own daily prayerful and meditative relationship with God, and a teacher of religion has something exceptional and unique from which to share.

Senior leadership positions in schools and parishes help with developing your relationship with God. These positions eventuated from the personal, academic background being based on Theology, Scripture, Liturgy and Religious Education, from experience gained in schools and through the personal spirituality being shared. Each qualification up to a master's degree has multiple levels of the areas covered. Whether you are leading a school as principal (two elementary/primary schools) or leading the religious school's religious aspect as an assistant principal or senior school levels as a Year Coordinator, you are exemplifying and living your relationship with God, your faith and beliefs. You are challenged daily with everyday human aspects of others' relationship with God, religion, the religious school, etc. Through all this, your relationship with God grows and strengthens.

Senior parish roles result in similar experiences to the religious school but on a parish or deanery level. (A deanery is a geographical grouping of various parishes. It by the leadership priest known as a Dean.) In my Chair of the parish or deanery roles, pastoral councils place you as a non-clergy leader, primarily of both the service and visionary aspects. You are there to help facilitate the spiritual, religious and pastoral growth of members of your parish or deanery. As a laity help for the priests. Through experiencing the challenges and goodness of all these people you deal with through these roles, you cannot help but be strongly influenced by their challenges, successes and failures in life and their relationships with God and each other. The influence this has on strengthening your relationship with God is substantial.

When you have an authentic, prayerful relationship with God, so much of God's truth becomes apparent. The impact is life-changing for the positive. You trust in God. God helps you through good and bad times. You have genuine compassion and empathy for humanity. God is indeed central to your existence. The commandment about placing God as number one across most religions becomes real and actual. You then naturally aim to love each other as God does. It is through this prayer and meditation lifestyle that you are more open to God and more prepared to discern God's messages for yourself and others. Discernment of God's messages becomes not just real, but an essential part of your life.

Karen, my wife of forty-two years, is integral to my relationship with God. Karen adds a depth needed to encounter God in these unique ways. She helps me understand and appreciate God's messages and Revelations through her unwavering support and openness to discuss each moment, each experience, each Tear from God encounter.

> …the need to accept my place in the scheme of God's plan and to go and do whatever is required to propagate the Revelation or message!
>
> … Each of these reasons supports the belief in either the Revelation or inspired messages

(Edited Extract from *Where's God? Revelations Today*, by Bryan Foster, 2018, p. 39-45.)

Appendix 5
Book 1 in 'GOD Today' Series

'1GOD.world: One GOD for ALL'

CONTENTS

PART 1

ONE GOD ONLY

Bryan Foster

Background Stories by Author

Appendix 6
Book 3 in 'GOD Today' Series

'Where's GOD? Revelations Today'

CONTENTS

PART 1

GOD'S REVELATION

PART 2 UNDERSTANDING GOD

GOD

Science

Suffering

Major World Changes Needed

Bryan Foster

Appendix 7

Book 4 in 'GOD Today' Series

'Where's GOD? Revelations Today Photobook Companion: GOD Signs (2nd ed)'

Outstanding and Unique sun and cloud images, mostly with the author receiving sun arrows, etc. Confused?

These need to be seen to be believed!

Author's Favourite Photobook and Book.

Introduction

Foreword

Unique Sun Formations

Easter Sun Crosses

Sun Arrows and Flares

Unique Sun Formations – Authenticity

Straddie Sun Arrows + Double Rainbow

Mt Warning Cloud – Rays Shooting Outwards

Revelations and Inspired Messages from GOD

Appendix 8
Book 5 in 'GOD Today' Series

Jesus and Mahomad* are GOD

Introduction   46

Author

Truths

Jesus and Mahomad* are GOD

ONE GOD - TWO INCARNATIONS   102

(*NB. The spelling of 'Mahomad' is deliberate. It is as
told by GOD to the author.)

21 REVELATIONS FOR TODAY

ESSENTIAL BACKGROUND APPENDICES

BIBLIOGRAPHY

Primary Source

GOD to the author

Secondary Sources

Websites

2016 *Census QuickStats: Tennant Creek*
http://www.censusdata.abs.gov.au/census_services/getprod
uct/census/2016/quickstat/SSC70251
2017 Series 18 *Heartbeat: The Miracle Inside You*, Dr Nikki
Stamp,
http://iview.abc.net.au/programs/catalyst/SC1602H005S00

http://www.abc.net.au/.../same-sex-marriage-survey-
ca.../8958176

http://www.abc.net.au/.../same-sex-marriage-survey-
ca.../8958176

ABS,
http://www.censusdata.abs.gov.au/census_services/getprod
uct/census/2016/quickstat/SSC70251

https://www.abs.gov.au/statistics/health/causes-
death/causes-death-australia/latest-release#intentional-self-
harm-suicide-in-aboriginal-and-torres-strait-islander-people

https://www.associationofcatholicpriests.ie/

Ali, A.H., 'Heretic: Why Islam Needs a Reformation Now'
https://www.goodreads.com/book/show/18669183-heretic

https://www.amazon.com/BryanFoster/e/B005DOPRMO/
ref=sr_tc_2_0?qid=1514764108&sr=1-2-ent

https://www.associationofcatholicpriests.ie

Ayaan's biography (seems entirely accurate from my readings)
https://en.wikipedia.org/wiki/Ayaan_Hirsi_Ali

https://www.caritas.org.au/learn/schools/just-visiting/cst-
for-best-practice
Catholic Social Teaching for Best Practice
https://www.caritas.org.au/learn/schools/just-visiting/cst-
for-best-practice
Census 2016: what's changed for Indigenous Australians?
https://theconversation.com/census-2016-whats-changed-
for-indigenous-australians-79836
Christine Roberts' (1967) song:
http://splash.abc.net.au/home#!/media/104826/?id=10482
6
Close the Gap Report on 'The Drum' 2/03/19
https://www.abc.net.au/news/2019-03-21/the-drum-
thursday-march-21/10927204

Drysdale, R., art examples:
https://www.artgallery.nsw.gov.au/collection/works/?artist_
id=drysdale-russell

Fishman, R., 2014, *No Man's Land,* Rising Tide Books, Sydney
– quote page 367.

http://www.rolandfishman.com.au/

Foster, B., Author, at https://www.bryanfosterauthor.com/ and https://godtodayseries.com

Foster, B., *Leo Downey's Buffalo Ranch*, Golden, BC, Canada - video https://www.youtube.com/watch?v=UCdA2UN5KqA

Foster, B., Leo Downey's, *Rocky Mountain Buffalo Ranch*, https://www.youtube.com/watch?v=UCdA2UN5KqA

Foster, B., YouTube channel (efozz1) – 780+ *'God Today' Series*, videos - Plus travel and *'How to caravan/trailer for beginners by Fozzie'* videos, at https://www.youtube.com/user/efozz1

https://www.facebook.com/MarianValleyShrine/

'GOD Today' Series
https://www.GODtodayseries.com/where-s-GOD

GOD Today Series on *Facebook*
https://www.facebook.com/groups/389602698051426/

http://leodowney.com/discography/leo-downey-2008/

http://leodowney.com/about-leo/ Madeline, 18-year-old from Canberra,

Leo Downey's *'The Rest of My Life'* at
https://www.youtube.com/watch?v=dS-OblC7c9M

Leo Downey at http://leodowney.com/about-leo/

Leonard Cohen's *'Hallelujah'* at
https://www.youtube.com/watch?v=YrLk4vdY28Q

Madeline, 18-year-old from Canberra,
http://www.theaustralian.com.au/.../9fb76f1b9f080a729aed ccb42...

http://marianvalley.org.au/

https://www.facebook.com/MarianValleyShrine/

'My Country' poem:
http://www.dorotheamackellar.com.au/archive/mycountry.h
tmhttp://www.dorotheamackellar.com.au/

Photobook Series by Bryan and Karen Foster
http://au.blurb.com/user/efozz1?profile_preview=true

Secularism -
https://www.google.com/search?q=secularism&rlz=1C1ZK
TG_enAU911AU911&oq=&aqs=chrome.0.69i59i450l8.1643
51852j0j15&sourceid=chrome&ie=UTF-8

Series 18 *Heartbeat: The Miracle Inside You*
https://iview.abc.net.au/video/SC1602H005S00

http://www.theaustralian.com.au/…/9fb76f1b9f080a729aed
ccb42…

Tennant Creek, NT - Drive Through video by Bryan Foster:
https://www.youtube.com/watch?v=PNsop7an73I

The Origins of Social Justice…
https://isi.org/intercollegiate-review/the-origins-of-social-
justice-taparelli-dazeglio/

http://theconversation.com/not-just-about-sex-throughout-
our-bodies-thousands-of-genes-act-differently-in-men-and-
women-86613

The executive director of The Sydney Institute.
https://www.catholicweekly.com.au/gerard-henderson-the-
media-the-commission-and-the-church/

What are human rights?
https://www.humanrights.gov.au/about/what-are-human-rights

Crystal Castle musical plants
https://www.youtube.com/watch?v=7U_z0MUo4MQ

Wujal Wujal, First Australian community, Far North Queensland
http://www.wujalwujalcouncil.qld.gov.au/

(All websites viewed 2020/1 unless otherwise stated.)

Books

Ali, A., *Why Islam Needs a Reformation Now*, 2016, Harper Collins, USA.

Downey, L., *Soultracker: Following Beauty*, 2014, Xlibris, USA.

Fishman, R., *No Man's Land*, 2014, Rising Tide Books, Sydney.

Foster, B., *1GOD.world: One GOD for All*, 2016, Great Developments Publishers, Gold Coast, Australia.

Foster, B., *Mt Warning GOD's Revelations: Photobook Companion to 1GOD.world*, 2017, Great Developments Publishers, Gold Coast, Australia.

Foster, B., *Where's GOD? Revelations Today*, 2018, Great Developments Publishers, Gold Coast, Australia.

Foster, B., *Where's GOD? Revelations Today Photobook Companion: GOD Signs*, 2018, Great Developments Publishers, Gold Coast, Australia.

Foster, B., *Jesus and Mahomad are GOD*, 2020, Great Developments Publishers, Gold Coast, Australia.

Tragic Face of Teenage Despair in The Australian, 21/3/19, NewsCorp, p.1.

*'Mahomad' is spelt as received from GOD directly in May, 2016.

Note

Bibliographic References - Variation

When searching the Bibliography or in-text references for specific research background details, you will observe the standard intext and bibliographic styles. You will also discover what I refer to as the Primary Revelation References, directly from GOD to me. This is stated at the beginning of the Bibliography.

Bibliography

Primary sources

GOD to the author

The primary reference for this book, *Jesus and Mahomad are GOD* and its series, *'GOD Today' Series,* is considerably different and unique from most other publications available worldwide today.

The Primary Revelation References are Revelations directly from GOD to me. These are not referenced from worldly publications, due to their nature and not being of this world's physical creation, but from the divine source. Each is as taken from GOD unless the details are stated otherwise.

It is the principal style used in Books 1, 3 and 5 from the *'GOD Today' Series.* Each reference becomes quite apparent in the various book articles, explanations and details. These may be direct Revelations from GOD or Inspired Messages from GOD or other forms of discerned vital points from GOD.

For example, let us consider the 21 Revelations, including Revelation #15, which is the title of this book, *Jesus and Mahomad are GOD*. Each of these 21 Revelations is directly from GOD and recorded by me on three separate occasions, 1982 (25th birthday – the starting day), 2016 and 2018 (Two camping venues around Mt Warning – Murwillumbah Showgrounds and ??? Mt Warning Caravan Park). The explanations of each Revelation have been discerned from GOD over the years. These were either as Inspired Messages or key discerned vital points explaining each Revelation.

Revelations appear to be 'spoken' by GOD, while Inspired Messages are 'felt/experienced' as from GOD. Vital points are primarily discerned and experienced as being known to be the Truth from GOD and significantly add to the details being inspired by GOD. These are more like daily information from GOD. These complete the necessary detail for appreciating GOD's Revelations, specific points and messages.

The Secondary References are as expected and as used by most everyday readers and academics. This is both for in-text referencing and the bibliography.

How are the similar words used in this Series?

Revelations appear to the receiver to be 'spoken' by God, through the 'mind's eye', (e.g. in the early morning hours for this author).

Inspired Messages are 'felt/experienced' as from God, (e.g. most are eventually written down or seen as reflections by this author).

Vital points are primarily discerned and experienced, often over longer periods of time, as being known to be the Truth from God and significantly add to the details being inspired by God. These are the 'everyday sort of information' from God to whomever requires God's assistance.

Index

Published by:

Great Developments Publishers

Gold Coast, Australia

Bryan Foster and Karen Foster - Directors

Copyright © 2008 - 2021 Great Developments Publishers

BOOKS BY AUTHOR

Books - Out Now

1GOD.world: One GOD for All, (Author Articles) (2016)

Mt Warning GOD's Revelation: Photobook Companion to '1GOD.world', (2017) (available at Apple & Blurb.com only)

Where's GOD? Revelations Today, (Author Articles) (2018)

Where's GOD? Revelations Today Photobook Companion: GOD Signs (2ⁿᵈed) (2018) ** (Spectacular, challenging, unique, authentic images from GOD.) **Author's favourite**.

Jesus and Mahomad are GOD (Author Articles) (2020)

Love is the Meaning of Life: GOD'S Love (1ˢᵗ ed) (Author Articles) (2021)

'GOD Today' Series (above) -

Images by Bryan Foster and Karen Foster (GDP), supported by Andrew Foster as advised (Austographer.com)

Photobooks - Out Now

'Straddie' North Stradbroke Island: Photobook of Natural & Shared Beauty, (2019)

Mt Warning Wollumbin Circuit: a photographic journey, (2018)

My Australia Photobooks Series – 12 x photobooks of Northern Territory, (FNQ) Far North Queensland, (2014-5) and 2 x Mt Warning, NSW (2017-8) by Bryan and Karen Foster

Marketing Books – School and Church - Out Now

School Marketing Manual for the Digital Age (3rd ed), (2008-1st, 2009-2nd, 2011-3rd)

Church Marketing Manual for the Digital Age (2nd ed), (2009-1st, 2011-2nd)

Books Coming

Love is the Meaning of Life (2nd ed) (Author Articles) (appr. 2021)

Wisdom made real: A lifetime of GODly hints and tips for us all (Author Articles) (appr. 2021/2) (Working Title)

Most photobooks were created from images taken while on our travels throughout Australia.

WEBSITES BY AUTHOR

For further information and reader response:

https://www.GODtodayseries.com/
-- Main website for this Series, includes the regularly updated blog commenced in 2016

https://www.jesusandmahomadareGOD.com/
- Book 5 (Coming Soon)

https://www.bryanfosterauthor.com/
- Author's website

https://loveisthemeaningoflifegodslove.com (Coming Soon)

https://loveisthemeaningoflife.com (Coming Soon)

http://www.greatdevelopmentspublishers.com/
- Publisher's new webpage. (Original website started in 2007, closed 12/2018. New webpage now.)

https://www.facebook.com/groups/389602698051426/
- 1GOD.world Facebook

https://au.linkedin.com/in/bryanfoster
- LinkedIn

https://www.youtube.com/user/efozz1
- 780+ YouTube videos commenced in 2009. Themes - 'GOD Today' Series. Caravan/trailer hints and tips for beginners. Places to see and things to do, mainly in Australia.

https://twitter.com/1GODworld1 -Twitter

https://www.instagram.com/
- Instagram (1GODworld) (Development stage)

Crucial Points in the

'GOD Today' Series (2016-2022)

Book 1. *1God.world: One God for All (Author Articles)* (2016)

The author's 25th birthday story – where this *Series* began.

God revealed fifteen Revelations to the author, Bryan Foster, in 2016. Bryan stayed in his caravan/trailer at the Murwillumbah Showgrounds, Australia, when God revealed these Revelations around 3 am on May 29, 2016. These were written down as 'spoken' by God, at God's request.

There is Only One God for all religions, cultures and people – for eternity.

'Tears from God' are real and highlight a unique closeness with God while communicating with God (e.g. Revelations, Inspired Messages, Prayer).

God loves everyone equally, no matter what.

Share stories of discovering God.

Science is a gift from God to be used wisely. To be used to help us know and appreciate God in our world. Then to use the knowledge found to improve our world and its people and all people's relationship with God and each other.

Don't blame God. Many actions by people cause a reaction which is unfair to God. Mostly it is people who cause the suffering or who don't react, and hence the suffering comes or continues. E.g. don't build on a geographic fault line if you don't want an earthquake. These are people's choices.

God loves Love, wilderness, beauty and humour for us all.

Forgiveness is often difficult, yet is essential for Love and communicating with God and those hurt by a person's sayings or actions.

Twenty-six author stories of his experience discovering God over his lifetime are shared.

God's simple messages and critical points for us all are shared.

Some Challenges and Solutions from God.

The Mt Warning/Wolumbin and Twelve Revelations' stories.

Book 2. *Mt Warning: God's Revelation Photobook Companion to '1God.world'* (2017)

Background images and story for Book 1.

Photographing Mt Warning from 360 degrees different angles.

I was driving the 72 km around and up to the walkers/climbers' Mt Warning starting point - the car park - three times over three days. Beautiful countryside, farms, state forest and national park. Inspired Book 1.

Growing closer to God, the further I drove around Mt Warning/Wolumbin.

Bryan Foster

Wolumbin is the local aboriginal, first people's name for Mt Warning, Australia.

God came from Heaven through a metaphorical 'conduit through Mt Warning' to the author in his caravan/trailer.

Only high-quality, original images are used. Many photos are quite spectacular.

Book 1 and Book 2 support and clarify each other.

Book 3. *Where's God? Revelations Today (Author Articles) (1st ed) (2018)*

God's Absolute Love and Equal Love for each of us is forever, past, present and future. Shared with billions of people over eternity.

Explanations of Revelations and Inspired Messages.

These Explanations are the Revealed Truth or the Discerned Truth from God.

The first twelve Revelations received from God are detailed.

God revealed six Inspired Messages in the last afternoon of receiving the twelve Revelations. These are now detailed for the reader.

Other Proof of the Truth examples. At this stage, the Sun is the basis for these. Book 4 following has numerous photographic sun examples from God. Many will surprise.

Understanding God – GOD, Love, Life & Death, Science, Suffering.

Significant world changes needed – Secular and Islamic. The western secular world needs to bring God back into it front, centre and strongly. Islam needs a Reformation, especially to stop the killings worldwide by the extreme, fundamentalist followers of Allah and Mahommed.

The author's story behind the Revelations and the direction taken for these to be disseminated worldwide.

Book 4, *Where's God? Revelations Today Photobook Companion: GOD's Signs (2ⁿᵈ ed)* is an integral part of Book 3's story. Key points to follow in Book 4, the next book analysed.

Book 4. *Where's God? Revelations Today Photobook Companion: GOD's Signs (2ⁿᵈ ed) (2018)*

This is the <u>author's favourite book in this *Series*</u>. The images are mostly unique and quite spectacular. Many will surprise and inspire the reader.

GOD's Signs emphasised here are based on Bryan's images and being of the author and the Sun.

Original images were taken at the foot of Mt Warning's car park for walkers/climbers. I was mostly using the Sun's shining rays through the rainforest canopy onto or near me and a physical copy of Book 3.

The uniqueness of images is quite unbelievable and spectacular.

The images weren't apparent while taking the photos and only became apparent when later uploaded to the laptop - most shots were taken on a Samsung mobile phone, some on a Panasonic pocket camera. (Devices are not being advertised here.)

These images are the Sun rays, sun flares, sun arrows, giant Easter sun cross and a double rainbow over the caravan.

Only good-quality original images are used in both Books 2 and 4. (Only one exception was used to help see the Sun's rays more clearly in a small cloud directly above Mt Warning. This image is on the cover of Book 2 and highlighted only when included in Book 4.)

The sun arrows are extra special. These are unbelievable until you accept each is genuine. A series of selfie-images taken a few seconds apart, show sun arrows moving from a flare from the Sun to me, either head or heart. Yet, check the book's written explanation and be very surprised at the direction of the sun-arrows.

These sun arrow images also occurred at other venues, including North Stradbroke Island, Kingscliff and Cabarita. Incidentally, all the places were within Mt Warning's original volcano's rim. The giant, spectacular Easter cross was taken at Texas on the NSW side of the Qld/NSW border, Australia, one week after Easter last year.

It is believed that God sent these to challenge the readers to go beyond any doubt they may have with these books' authenticity. The images are very different from what often has probably been seen by most, if not all, of the readers.

Book 5. *Jesus and Mahomad are God (Author Articles) (2020)*

Both Jesus and Mahomad* are God's Incarnations.

* ('Mahomad' spelt this way in the Revelations from God to me.)

Mahomad and Jesus are both God. God and Allah are both the same God.

God desires for Islam to make significant changes, especially so that violence will be illuminated.

Former Muslim, Ayaan Hirsi Ali in her 2015's book *Heretic: Why Islam Needs a Reformation Now* highlights this and other Islam beliefs. Ayaan was born in Somalia, became a politician in the Netherlands and is now a former Senior Fellow, The Future of Diplomacy Project, Harvard University, USA.

The author was invited directly by God to be a prophet one Saturday night while with Karen, my wife, at home. I am still working through this? Feel like I have accepted it, but still doubtful. Time will tell. This is a most challenging request, yet probably more familiar than many would have anticipated.

The last six Revelations from the twenty-one are finalised here in Book 5 - Along with details about Revelations #6, #13, #14.

The critical beliefs sent by God here are: We Need God; Be vulnerable to God; Be continually requesting God's help; Fully accept that we are insignificant compared to God; God is so superior-stop fighting over God; Be genuinely meek, humble and truly real.

Appendices in Book 5 include several background key points for the reader who likes a quick refresher of previous books in the *Series*, as they read Book 5.

Book 6. *Love is the Meaning of Life: GOD's Love (Author Articles) (1ˢᵗ ed.) (2021)*

What is Love? - Love is so much more than, 'I love you.'

GOD Is Absolute Love.

GOD Loves Each of Us Equally.

Loving GOD needed now more than ever

NEEDING GOD

Experiencing GOD Directly

Revelations for Today's World - 1 to 21 from GOD to

Author – an Overview in 2016 and 2018

Life is Not Fair. You Can't Have Everything.

GOD's Love and Forgiveness

Forgiveness

GOD said, 'Love One Another as I have loved you.'

All Humans, all Fauna, all Flora are Soul-filled and Pure at birth + have an Eternal Choice to Make at Death (Author's view)

Old-Age and GOD

Priests, Pastors and other Religious Leaders from all Genuine Religions - Don't Ignore these GOD's Messengers. Their Love for their congregations and communities is outstanding and needs our support.

Music from GOD. Two Exceptional Musicians examples - Canadians - Leo Downey and Leonard Cohen (The Late)

Religious Challenges

Social Justice and Human Rights

Perfection?

Media is Relatively Silent on GOD Today

Social Media Becoming Essential for Religions and Religious Leaders

Secularism is Dangerous and Hollow - possibly Leading

Humanity to a Catastrophe

Religious Solutions

Perfection vs Non-Perfection

Forgiveness is Godliness

Angels Exist + Evil Exists on Earth and in Hell, but not the Devil (Author)

Author's Teaching and Religious/Church Experience – 42 years teaching religion - includes 30 years teaching Study of Religion to years 11 and 12.My Retirement Last Lesson – 'Tears from God' from most present

Book 7. *Love is the Meaning of Life (Author Articles) (2ⁿᵈ ed.) (2021)* (Working Copy)

What is Love? A Different Perspective Without God

Love is the Meaning of Life

Love and Forgiveness – Essential for Authentic Love

Love in Nature, e.g. Oceanic Dolphins or Bushlands

Love is Giving, Especially During Catastrophes

Humans Feel the Same Inherently Until…

Gifted, Talented and Fortunate OWE the World Out of Love

Love's Challenges

Human Frailties Affect Loving Relationships

Physical Perfection

Abuse is Never Right

Differences Between Male and Female Psyches

Coherent Family Structures

In particular, World Security Needs the Young to Appreciate What's Happening in the World – the News!

Indigenous Worldwide Often Lack Real Hope

Hate Speech

Love's Solutions

What Does GOD have to do With Love? Could there be a decent argument for GOD Being Real along with Positive Links to Love?

Loving Not Abusive Relationships

Gentle Empathetic, Males

Coherent Family Structures

True Feminism

Women are People First Female Second – And Beautiful Creations

Need Integrated Leadership Models of Males and Females

Treating Each Other Equally

A Country's First People Need Hope, Love, Acceptance, Forgiveness and Assistance from the whole Community. With Their Views Being the Dominant in Discussions and Final Decisions. The non-indigenous, in Particular, must be respectful and Loving in all dealings…

Book 8. *Wisdom of Love: Wisdom of GOD's Love (Author Articles) (Working Copy & Title) (2021/2)*

Content for this Book 9 is currently being explored. There are already 130 wise statements to be included. The list is growing by the day. These have been forming for the author over the past years, right up until now. Each is an Inspired Message from GOD.

Book 9. *Love is the Meaning of Life GOD's Love: Photobook Companion (2021/2) (Working Draft)*

A photobook companion to the two *Love is the Meaning of Life* (1st and 2nd Editions) – i.e. Books 6 and 7 from *'GOD Today' Series*. Some exceptional and unique images will help highlight and tie together the key points of both books. These also highlight relevant and linked topics throughout the *Series*. Key issues will be explained as required so that no clarity is lost. This is the third photobook companion in the *Series*.

'GOD Today' Series -

Books available from all good internet bookstores and various local bookshops and libraries.

e-books are available from Amazon, Apple and Blurb -

(except Book 2, a photobook, which is only available from Apple and Blurb)

Bryan Foster